PEOPLE'S CHINA AT 75
– THE FLAG STAYS RED

Edited by *Keith Bennett* and *Carlos Martinez*

PRAXIS PRESS

PEOPLE'S CHINA AT 75 – THE FLAG STAYS RED

Edited by *Keith Bennett* and *Carlos Martinez*

Print edition: 978-1-899155-39-2

Published by Praxis Press 2025
Email: praxispress@me.com
Website: www.redletterspp.com

This book is published to celebrate the first 75 years of the People's Republic of China. **Praxis Press** gratefully acknowledges the support of **Friends of Socialist China** – a platform based on supporting the PRC and spreading understanding of Chinese socialism. Homepage: socialistchina.org

Content copyright remains with the individual authors. Design and layout with Praxis Press.

Praxis Press
c/o 26 Alder Road
Glasgow, G43 2UU
Scotland, Great Britain

CONTENTS

	Introduction: Understanding socialism with Chinese characteristics *Keith Bennett* and *Carlos Martinez*	v
1	Building socialism with Chinese characteristics *Ken Hammond*	1
2	China's transition to socialism: 1949-1956 *Jenny Clegg*	13
3	Standing up, living long, opposing hegemony *Andrew Murray*	27
4	The significance of China's fulfilment of its Second Centenary Goal by 2049 *Cheng Enfu* and *Chen Jian*	39
5	The 'primary stage of socialism' in historical context *Kenny Coyle*	51
6	China's socialist democracy *Roland Boer*	65
7	Common prosperity *Mick Dunford*	75
8	Mao, China, and the development of Marxism-Leninism *J. Sykes*	91

9	Building socialism, building the ecological civilisation	101
	Efe Can Gürcan	
10	Patient finance: Beijing's core challenge to the Washington Consensus	117
	Radhika Desai	
11	How China survived the end of history	133
	Carlos Martinez	
	Contributors	150

Introduction
Understanding socialism with Chinese characteristics

Keith Bennett and Carlos Martinez

No blueprint for the building of socialism
THE COMMUNIST MANIFESTO, the foundational text of scientific socialism, is still considerably short of 200 years old. Meanwhile, the working class and its allies have now held state power, and engaged in a serious project of socialist nation-building, for little over a century.

The Chinese working class, together with the peasantry and representatives of all patriotic sections of Chinese society, have held state power for 75 years, with some two decades of administering revolutionary base areas before that.

Since the October Revolution of 1917, serious attempts, with varying degrees of success, have been made to establish and build socialism in Europe, Asia, the Caribbean, South America and Africa.

Thus on the one hand we can say that humanity has acquired a certain degree of experience and lessons, both positive and negative, regarding the struggle to establish and build socialism. But more fundamentally, we can say that, in the long course of human history, socialism remains a very new and fledgling system.

This is not to say that there is nothing to learn and draw from. Xi Jinping's point that socialism with Chinese characteristics offers "a new option for other countries and nations who want to speed up their development while preserving their independence" acquires ever greater validity practically with each passing day.[1]

And communists everywhere still draw on the historical experience of the USSR, its monumental achievements – and mistakes – as well as the experience of every historical and contemporary attempt to build socialism.

But despite the fact that we do not start from a completely blank page, the most fundamental lesson we can draw so far from the historical and ongoing attempts to build socialism is that there is no ready-made blueprint or master plan, no straight road, and certainly no 'one size fits all' formula that can be downloaded and implemented at any time and in any place.

Moreover, for most of their political lives (arguably less so towards the end) Marx and Engels envisaged socialism replacing highly developed and advanced capitalism. So far, this has not happened anywhere.

One could of course argue, like some ultra-leftists and dogmatists, that this somehow invalidates the whole experience of actually existing socialism. Or one can appreciate that this conditions the context in which countries and peoples move towards socialism; that every country will approach socialism in its own way; and that, not least, the character and duration of the transition period may vary enormously.

What is highly relevant to those countries in which socialism has actually triumphed, theorised by Lenin as "breaking the chain at its weakest link",[2] is the fact that attempts to build socialism have all occurred in a world that is still largely dominated by capitalism and imperialism.

Moreover, every preceding class that rose to political power did so in the context of their rapidly developing economic power. In the case of the proletariat, it is almost the exact opposite.

All this helps explain why Stalin, in his *Foundations of Leninism*, explains that, "the bourgeoisie that is overthrown in one country remains for a long time stronger than the proletariat which has overthrown it".[3]

This is some of the context in which we must start to look at the trajectory of the Chinese revolution.

Although China has the world's longest continuous civilisation and was the world's biggest economy for most of the last two millennia, since the British launched the first Opium War in 1839, the country was reduced to a semi-colonial, semi-feudal society. Not for nothing is the ensuing period known by the Chinese as the 'century of humiliation', marked by unequal treaties, foreign aggression – most devastatingly that by Japan in the 1930s and 1940s – and by wars of aggression and resistance, civil wars and ultimately a victorious revolution.

When the People's Republic of China was proclaimed in 1949, China was one of the poorest and most wretched societies on earth. Illiteracy was as high as life expectancy was low.

UNDERSTANDING SOCIALISM WITH CHINESE CHARACTERISTICS

Revolutionary successes

So, how did the Chinese revolution succeed?

Stalin and Trotsky quarrelled bitterly over the course of the Chinese revolution (as indeed they quarrelled bitterly about many things), but neither of them conceived what was probably Mao Zedong's single greatest contribution to the application and development of Marxism: namely that in a large, semi-colonial, semi-feudal country, as China was at the time, the revolution could be won, and the path to socialism opened up, with a Marxist-Leninist party representing and embodying working class political leadership, but with the peasantry – in accordance with the country's demographics, social system and class composition – playing the main role, by basing the revolutionary forces in the countryside, building stable revolutionary base areas, waging a protracted people's war, surrounding the cities from the countryside and ultimately seizing nationwide political power by armed force.[4]

This strategic innovation by Mao constitutes the beginning of the Sinification of Marxism and the most fundamental root of socialism with Chinese characteristics. It is also the model that was essentially applied to the revolution in countries as varied as Vietnam, Laos, Cambodia, Yugoslavia, Albania, Cuba, Mozambique, Zimbabwe, Eritrea, and Guinea Bissau, among others.

Two distinct phases

The subsequent political trajectory of the People's Republic – of course with many sub themes and caveats – essentially divides into two distinct phases.

The first of these phases is the period from the PRC's founding in 1949 until the launch of *Reform and Opening Up* in 1978, two years after the death of Mao.

This phase is often described as following the Soviet model. There is some truth to this; indeed China's first five-year plan (1953–1957) was influenced to a significant degree by the Soviet development strategy, and Soviet assistance played an important role in fulfilling it. As in the Soviet Union, there was very little role for markets or for private enterprise (albeit the transformation to a publicly-owned economy in China took place over several years and was largely peaceful).

Nonetheless, to describe the Mao era as "following the Soviet model" does not tell the full story.

Firstly, even in its most radical phases, the Chinese revolution never completely rejected a role for the national bourgeoisie. This in turn meant that, rather than a single party system, as in the Soviet Union, China retained, and retains, a multi-party, consultative system, based on acknowledging and upholding the leading role of the Communist Party.

There was always greater scope for local autonomy in applying and implementing national policies, and greater possibility for mass participation and initiative – phenomena which largely withered away in the Soviet Union after the first generation of socialist construction.

Above all, the peasantry (with some deviation during the Great Leap Forward, 1958-62), was not taken as a source of what might be termed 'socialist primitive accumulation' to benefit the proletariat in the cities and the promotion of heavy industry. Rather, policies were if anything skewed in favour of the countryside, reflecting the fact that the peasantry constituted the majority of the population, the bedrock of the revolution, and the core of the party's support.

The achievements of the Mao era should not be underestimated or denigrated. They were among the most remarkable in human history.

Despite the terrible years of 1958-62, and the chaos of the Cultural Revolution, life expectancy in China grew by one year for every year that Mao was in power. From being practically the poorest country on earth, China solved the basic problems of feeding, clothing, housing and educating a fifth of the world's population; provided basic medical care to the whole population; brought literacy to the overwhelming majority of the population; and massively improved the social position and role of women. The pre-revolution literacy rate in China was less than 20 percent; by the time Mao died, it was 93 percent. China's population had remained stagnant between 400 and 500 million for a hundred years or so up to 1949; by the time Mao died, it had reached 900 million. A thriving culture of literature, music, theatre and art grew up that was accessible to the masses of the people. Famine became a thing of the past. Universal healthcare was established. Crucially, China maintained its sovereignty and developed the means to defend itself from imperialist attack.

From 1978, the post-Mao Chinese leadership embarked on a process of Reform and Opening Up: gradually introducing market mechanisms to the economy, allowing elements of private property, and encouraging investment from the capitalist world. This programme posited that, while China had established a socialist society, it would remain for some time in the primary stage of socialism, during which period it was necessary to develop a socialist market economy – combining planning, the development of a mixed economy and the profit motive – with a view to maximising the development of the productive forces.

Why was such a radical turn considered necessary?

For all its unprecedented progress, China remained at the time of Mao's death a very poor country. Per capita GDP was lower than that of sub-Saharan Africa, although, of course, the 'social wage' was considerably higher, and even the poor had secure access to land and housing – by which measure they were doing much better than most of their counterparts in the developing world.

Although the basic necessities of life were more or less guaranteed, most people remained very poor. Whilst famine had been eliminated, food was strictly rationed and monotonous, and food insecurity remained a constant worry. Eggs, let alone meat, were a considerable luxury. Xi Jinping, when recalling his young days working with farmers in an old revolutionary base area, has often said that his dream was that one day the villagers would be able to eat meat and to eat it often.[5] In his time there, they might have tasted meat once or twice a year.

Although disparities and inequalities obviously remained, China under Mao may be considered to have been one of the most equal societies on earth. However, it also remained one of the poorest. This is what Deng Xiaoping was alluding to when he said that universal poverty is not socialism and that, "to uphold socialism, a socialism that is to be superior to capitalism, it is imperative first and foremost to eliminate poverty".[6]

Moreover, huge changes were underway, both in the region around China and in the world. Science and technology were rapidly developing and revolutionising the productive forces. Countries and regions around China were developing rapidly – albeit inequitably and for specific reasons, including imperialism's desire to have 'showcases' on the borders or vicinity of China, the DPRK and Vietnam and to fend off any further local communist challenges in a region with a strong tradition of armed communist resistance.

Chinese economist Justin Yifu Lin notes that, at the time of the founding of the PRC, there was only a relatively small per capita income gap between China and its East Asian neighbours:

> But by 1978 Japan had basically caught up with the United States, and South Korea and Taiwan, China, had narrowed the income gap with developed countries. China, although boasting a complete industrial system, an atomic bomb, and a man-made satellite, had a standard of living a far cry from that of the developed world.[7]

Thousands of Chinese were undertaking the perilous swim in the hope of securing a better life in Hong Kong.

The capitalist development in East and South-East Asia was skilfully turned into a positive factor by China as its principal source of investment in the first stage of Reform and Opening Up. The eagerness of investors to enter the Chinese market had a number of causes, including the patriotism – and attachment to ancestral homes – of much of the Chinese bourgeoisie in Hong Kong, Macau, Taiwan and throughout South-East Asia and beyond; awareness of the size and potential of the Chinese market; the US defeat in Vietnam and partial retreat from Asia; and a cynical desire to perpetuate and exacerbate the Sino-Soviet split.

For China, investment, initially largely from overseas Chinese and soon more generally, was crucial. It provided what the country desperately needed: a faster pace of industrialisation and employment for those leaving the countryside to begin urban life; guaranteed export markets; skills and technology transfer; capital; technical and vocational training and skills uplift; and advanced and scientific management, something with which Lenin was famously enamoured, writing in 1918: "The Soviet Republic must at all costs adopt all that is valuable in the achievements of science and technology… The possibility of building socialism depends exactly upon our success in combining the Soviet power and the Soviet organisation of administration with the up-to-date achievements of capitalism. We must organise in Russia the study and teaching of the Taylor system and systematically try it out and adapt it to our own ends."[8]

No Great Wall

None of China's economic reform would have been possible – at least not on the same scale, to the same extent and at such a rapid pace – without the foundations laid during the Mao period: a basically educated, literate and trained workforce; housing; medical care; a transportation network; paved roads linking the whole country; and so on. As the late Egyptian Marxist Samir Amin commented, the post-1978 period "would not have been possible without the economic, political and social foundations that had been built up in the preceding period"[9] – a period which achieved, in the words of Deng Xiaoping himself, "progress on a scale which old China could not achieve in hundreds or even thousands of years".[10]

That is why even today, talk of companies like Apple or Foxconn simply upping sticks from China and relocating en bloc to India, for example, remains largely fanciful.

Another crucially important factor laying the foundations for the reform process was the relatively stable international environment, in particular China's improved relations with the leading capitalist countries. It was the re-establishment of relations between the US and China from 1972, and China's accession to the UN in 1971, that transformed China's international environment and laid the ground for developing trade links with, and absorbing technological expertise from, the capitalist world. As such, the first steps of *opening up* can be considered to have been guided by Mao Zedong and Zhou Enlai.

These continuities are a major reason why Xi Jinping, right from practically his first remarks when he was elected General Secretary of the party in 2012, has consistently stressed that the two phases of China's socialist development should not be counterposed to one another, but rather be seen as two parts of a single revolutionary whole, one resting on the foundations laid by the other.

> Although the two historical phases are very different in their guiding thoughts, principles, policies, and practical work,

they are by no means separated from or opposed to each other. We should neither negate the pre-reform-and-opening-up phase in comparison with the post-reform-and-opening-up phase, nor the converse.[11]

In this, it must be said, he fundamentally differs both from standard bourgeois analyses but also from those who take up different positions on the left to slight or denigrate one or other phase of China's socialist development.

Deng Xiaoping intuitively grasped that if you could deploy market mechanisms to unleash the enthusiasm and skills of the people, China would rapidly develop and people's living standards would increase. Once farmers were given extensive freedom to grow and cultivate what they chose, and to sell their surplus, in just a couple of years, food supply went from rationed and precarious to abundant and diverse.

If growth in the Mao period was, taken as a whole, steady, once reform and opening up got underway, it became turbo-charged. From being a poor country, marginal to the global economy, China has become the world's second largest economy (the largest if measured by Purchasing Power Parity). China is the world's biggest manufacturer, largest exporter, and biggest trading partner for the majority of nations. It has rocketed up the value chain, increasingly leading the world in innovation and R&D, with the largest number of new patents and peer reviewed articles in scientific journals.

In just a few years, the whole country was covered in a network of high-speed rail. China is leading the world in tackling climate change, from solar panels to electric vehicles.[12] And now China is leading in the development of new, high quality productive forces, essentially conforming to the fifth industrial revolution.

People's democratic dictatorship

It has to be stressed that, whilst promoting extensive economic liberalisation, Deng Xiaoping was completely resolute in defending what he called the Four Cardinal Principles, namely the dictatorship of the proletariat (generally referred to as the people's democratic dictatorship in the conditions of China), the socialist road, the leadership of the Communist Party, and Marxism-Leninism and Mao Zedong Thought.[13]

It is a simple fact that, under the leadership of Deng Xiaoping, an attempt at counter-revolution in China in 1989 was resolutely crushed, whereas in the same year, counter-revolution triumphed in almost the whole of Eastern Europe, and two years later in the Soviet Union itself. In a critical period, it is not an exaggeration to say that Deng Xiaoping, along with his veteran comrades like Chen Yun – as well as the leaders of the Democratic People's Republic of Korea, Cuba, Vietnam and Laos – literally saved world socialism. As Deng said in a talk with Tanzania's Julius Nyerere in 1989, "so long as socialism does not collapse in China, it will always hold its ground in the world."[14]

Of course, no change as rapid and radical, and on so vast a canvas, as the process of Reform and Opening Up in China could possibly unfold without, as a secondary aspect, some serious negative features. Whilst everyone, or very nearly everyone, in the long run, and not discounting some painful periods for many, has become much better off, what was once probably the world's most equal society has become highly unequal. This has also included regional disparities and between town (where the majority of Chinese people now live) and country, and between migrant workers and others.

Massive damage was done to the environment and ideological and political work weakened.

This in a sense was prefigured by Premier Zhou Enlai, albeit in the customary Chinese form of reviewing history, when, in his report to the 10th Party Congress in August 1973, he observed that in the course of the Chinese revolution, one tendency had always covered another.[15] That is, leftist deviations had occurred in the course of correcting right opportunism and vice versa.

The New Era

This is essentially what Xi Jinping has been working tirelessly to correct since he assumed the leadership in 2012, inaugurating what the Chinese now call the New Era. Among its key features are:

- A merciless and ceaseless campaign against corruption, both the major variety that inflicts damage on the country as a whole and the petty kind that can inflict misery on ordinary people. Or as the Chinese say, targeting both tigers and flies.

- A rectification of the party's ranks, strengthening its ties to the people and decisively returning to the concept of serving the people.

- A massive, targeted campaign resulting in the historically unprecedented elimination of extreme poverty, with careful follow-up to ensure that people do not slip back into poverty and that their lives continue to improve.

- Tackling pollution, preserving the environment, safeguarding biodiversity, leading the world in renewable energy, building an ecological civilisation at home, and leading the global fight against climate catastrophe.

- Rolling out by far the world's largest programme of medical care and insurance, and old age pensions, albeit ones that remain in many respects rudimentary and with great scope for improvement.

- Ensuring that all sectors of the economy, including the privately-owned sectors, work in the overall interests of socialism. In the private sector, relevant measures include far greater regulation of the technology sector and now the property and real estate sector; the taking of golden shares, partial ownership, or seats on the board of major private companies by the party and state; the organisation of party committees to exercise a supervisory role in private firms; and unionisation of the workforce.[16]

- A reaffirmation of the central and guiding role of Marxism.

- Deng Xiaoping's policy of keeping a low profile and not taking the lead in international affairs has been superseded by a more proactive foreign policy, addressing all the key questions of the current world situation, and with the strategic goal of building a community of shared future for humanity.[17]

- Increased support for the other socialist countries and a more dynamic engagement with the international communist movement as a whole.

Whilst China remains, in its own words, in the primary stage of socialism, the overall goal is now to build a "great modern socialist country that is prosperous, strong, democratic, culturally advanced, harmonious and beautiful" by the centenary of the PRC's founding in 2049.[18]

It is worth noting, as Andrew Murray does in his chapter in this volume, that People's China has now survived for longer than the Soviet state. Survival in a world still dominated by imperialism has always been, and remains, a real issue for socialist countries. Lenin is said to have danced in the snow when the October Revolution survived for longer than the Paris Commune. Similarly, we should rejoice in the longevity and resilience of the People's Republic as it marks its 75th anniversary.

Returning to the starting point of this introduction, there is no ready-made formula, special secret, or royal road for building socialism, not in China or in any other country. We are not in solidarity with this or that particular policy at any given time. Time, social practice and the Chinese people will judge them – as Xi Jinping often says, "only the wearer of the shoes knows if they fit or not".[19]

We are in solidarity with what we support in every country without exception: a better and more dignified life for working people; a cause that finds its highest expression in the socialist countries, the countries where the working class and its allies are organised as the ruling class, and which we must defend through thick and thin, come what may and without reservation, if humanity is to have a future.

NOTES

1. Xi Jinping 2017, *Full text of Xi Jinping's report at 19th CPC National Congress*, China Daily. https://www.chinadaily.com.cn/china/19thcpcnationalcongress/2017-11/04/content_34115212.htm
2. VI Lenin 1917, *The Chain Is No Stronger Than Its Weakest Link*, Marxist Internet Archive. https://www.marxists.org/archive/lenin/works/1917/may/27.htm
3. JV Stalin 1924, *The Foundations of Leninism (chapter 4)*, Marxist Internet Archive. https://www.marxists.org/reference/archive/stalin/works/1924/foundations-leninism/ch04.htm
4. This theme is explored further in J Sykes' contribution to this volume, *Mao, China, and the Development of Marxism-Leninism*
5. *Xi Focus: 'I was once a farmer'*, China Daily. https://www.chinadaily.com.cn/a/202203/07/WS62256dc4a310cdd39bc8ad3b.html
6. Deng Xiaoping 1987, *To Uphold Socialism We Must Eliminate Poverty*, Marxist Internet Archive. https://www.marxists.org/reference/archive/deng-xiaoping/1987/133.htm
7. Justin Yifu Lin, *Demystifying the Chinese Economy*, Cambridge University Press, Cambridge, 2012, p153
8. VI Lenin 1918, *The Immediate Tasks of the Soviet Government*, Marxist Internet Archive. https://www.marxists.org/archive/lenin/works/1918/mar/x03.htm
9. Samir Amin. *Beyond US Hegemony: Assessing the Prospects for a Multipolar World*, Zed Books, United Kingdom, 2013, p23
10. Deng Xiaoping 1979, *Uphold the four cardinal principles*, China Daily. https://www.chinadaily.com.cn/china/19thcpcnationalcongress/2010-10/15/content_29714546.htm
11. Xi Jinping 2014, *The Governance of China*, Foreign Languages Press, Beijing, p61
12. As detailed in Efe Can Gürcan's contribution to this volume, *Building Socialism, Building the Ecological Civilisation: China's Revolutionary Path to Sustainable Development*
13. Deng Xiaoping 1979, *Uphold the four cardinal principles*, China Daily. https://www.chinadaily.com.cn/china/19thcpcnationalcongress/2010-10/15/content_29714546.htm
14. Deng Xiaoping 1989, *We Must Adhere To Socialism and Prevent Peaceful Evolution Towards Capitalism*, Marxist Internet Archive. https://www.marxists.org/reference/archive/deng-xiaoping/1989/173.htm
15. Zhou Enlai 1973, *Report to the Tenth National Congress of the Communist Party of China*, Marxist Internet Archive. https://www.marxists.org/subject/china/documents/cpc/10th_congress_report.htm

16 Much of this is discussed in Michael Dunford's chapter, *Common Prosperity*.

17 Xi Jinping 2017, *Work Together to Build a Community of Shared Future for Mankind*, Xinhua. http://www.xinhuanet.com/english/2017-01/19/c_135994707.htm

18 *Xi unveils plan to make China "great modern socialist country" by mid-21st century*, Xinhua. http://www.xinhuanet.com/english/2017-10/18/c_136688933.htm

19 Xi Jinping, *The Governance of China. 3. First edition*, Foreign Languages Press, Beijing, 2020, p150

1

Building socialism with Chinese characteristics

Ken Hammond

It has become a commonplace of contemporary Chinese political discourse to speak of socialism with Chinese characteristics [*zhongguo tese shehui zhuyi* 中國特色社會主義]. Often viewed as having originated as a specific phrasing used by Deng Xiaoping on September 1, 1982, in a speech at the 12th National Congress of the Communist Party of China (CPC), it has been elaborated by subsequent leaders and developed in academic circles over the past four decades. Each volume of Xi Jinping's The Governance of China begins with a section devoted to the concept. The term is included in the constitution of the CPC. Western pundits and politicians often mock China's political rhetoric as opaque or convoluted as a way of dismissing the ideas of socialism or the achievements of economic development in China. For many ordinary people not familiar with the conventions of political language in China, terms such as this can indeed be difficult to understand. Yet the concept of socialism with Chinese characteristics is critical to an accurate appraisal of China's political economy and society today. How can this idea be made more comprehensible for Western audiences?

At its most basic level, the phrase "with Chinese characteristics" simply modifies the noun socialism. But in a sense, this only complicates things, because then we must begin with what socialism means, and this has been a contentious topic of debate for a couple of centuries. For our purposes, though, this is actually a rather fruitful ambiguity. Because the substance of the concept of socialism with Chinese characteristics is exactly the dynamic, dialectical process of developing both a theoretical model and practical applications of the process of creating a new socialist economy and society in China, not as the simple building out of a template or blueprint of a universal phenomenon called socialism, but as the specific adaptation and development of the analytical methods of historical materialism as developed by Marx, Engels, Lenin, and others in the course of revolutionary history, and the experience gathered in the course of struggles against capitalism and imperialism, to the material conditions and historical realities of China. This has not come about in a single moment or as a pre-determined process, but has emerged over the past century of revolutionary struggle in China. Indeed, the historical trajectory of China's development, of the experience of socialist construction as it has been pursued over the past 75 years, can only be understood as the living practice of the dialectical method, the working out of how to use the analytical insights of historical materialism as a means of grasping the specificity of conditions in China, and to shape the course of development in accordance with that reality. It is this trajectory that I want to trace here.

The challenge of adapting Marxism to the actual material and social conditions of China goes back to the very establishment of the CPC in 1921. The founders, and the advisers sent by the Communist International (Comintern) who assisted in the process of bringing the party into being, initially viewed China from a theoretical perspective strongly shaped by classical European Marxist ideas. Because China had a very small industrial working class, they came to view the situation as being not ripe for a proletarian revolution. Instead, they focused on working with the Guomindang (GMD), the Nationalist Party, which was viewed as the vehicle for carrying through a bourgeois anti-imperialist revolution which would then set the stage for a period of economic development. Only when this had been carried through would conditions be ready for a proletarian revolution. In the early 1920s the CPC and GMD did indeed form a united front, but this ended in disaster for the communists in 1927 when Chiang Kai-shek (Jiang Jieshi) split with the CPC and launched a major campaign of murder and arrests that decimated the party. Even after this the Comintern and many in the party leadership maintained their view that there was not a sufficient basis for a socialist-led revolution.

But it was during these years that Mao Zedong, who had joined the GMD as part of the united front, carried out his investigations into conditions in the countryside, working with peasant unions and analysing the class nature of rural society. He came to understand that China's agricultural sector was heavily commercialised, as it had been for centuries, and that much rural economic production and circulation was capitalist; a distinctive form of commercial capitalism possessing all the features of capitalist production Marx had outlined in *Capital* and other writings. Mao had the insight to see that a significant proportion of workers on the land constituted what he called, in his "Report on an Investigation of the Peasant Movement in Hunan" and in other writings, the rural proletariat. This insight provided the key to the path of revolutionary struggle in China. Marx had seen peasants in France and elsewhere in Europe as petit-bourgeois, and vulnerable to align their interests with the ruling class. But in China, Mao understood, conditions were different, and the great majority of peasants would be the driving force of the anti-imperialist and anti-capitalist movement.

Mao continued to promote these ideas in other writings and through the investigation of actual material conditions in different parts of China. In May 1930 he drafted his essay "On the Work of Investigation", which was later re-titled "Oppose Book Worship," in which he argued strongly for the necessity of this kind of analytical work, seeking truth from facts and not relying on pre-existing theoretical models without testing their applicability to the real world. This is the fundamental meaning of the idea of socialism with Chinese characteristics, socialism adapted to and suitable for the actually existing conditions of the country.

His ideas did not attain immediate acceptance by the party leadership. The advisers from the Comintern continued to hold to a line that saw the industrial workers as the only legitimate proletarian force. But slowly, through the success of the political and social experiments carried on in the Jiangxi Soviet in the early 1930s, Mao's views came to be embraced by other leaders, and in January 1935, in the early days of the Long March, a conference was held during a pause in the town of Zunyi in Guizhou province, at which Mao's perspective was recognised as the correct approach for China. From that point on Mao became the effective leader of the revolution. He continued to develop his theoretical insights, which he elaborated in writings like "On Contradiction" and "On Practice" as well as in many works devoted to the analysis of specific circumstances and conditions which would shape the course of the struggle. In all these instances Mao sought to apply Marx's methods to Chinese realities, rather than treating his texts as some kind of scriptural authority.

With Liberation and the establishment of the People's Republic in 1949 the real work of socialist construction, with the ongoing need to fit Marxist theory to Chinese realities, could begin. The 75-year history of the PRC can be divided into three distinct periods, in each of which the adaptation of Marxist theory to actual Chinese conditions was carried forward, in various ways. The first period, from 1949-1978, was one in which the Communist Party struggled to determine the best path forward, with diverging views of agricultural collectivisation, industrial development, and other issues manifesting themselves in what is often referred to as the "struggle between two lines." A second phase began when Deng Xiaoping assumed the leading role in the party at the end of 1978 and launched the program of reform and opening to the outside. The years from 1979 until 2011 saw China make rapid progress in economic development and undergo dramatic transformations in social life. But this also entailed a degree of accommodation with the global capitalist system centred on the United States, as China sought to acquire investment, technologies of production, and other knowledge from the outside to accelerate the process of socialist construction. The third period, which continues to the present day, began with the election of Xi Jinping in 2012. This current era has been one in which China, having achieved a sufficient level of social accumulation, has been more self-confident and less willing to acquiesce to the waning power of the U.S. and its vassal allies. Each of these periods will be discussed in what follows.

The various players in the first act of this drama, including Mao Zedong and Zhou Enlai, Liu Shaoqi and Deng Xiaoping and many others, all shared the objective of pursuing socialist development, but they developed very different views of how best to do that. Mao and those associated with him gave relatively more emphasis to mass participation and the overriding need for the party to be closely linked to the people, while Liu, Deng, and others focused more on the technical and managerial challenges of creating new systems of production and distribution as well as scientific and technological issues, and often saw those with specialised expertise as playing the leading role in the process of development.

The first thirty years of the People's Republic saw many significant achievements. The country was made stable and secure, life expectancy significantly increased, while infant mortality declined. The provision of housing, health care, education, and other social services was basically guaranteed. On average over these years the economy grew by around 3% annually. Yet even with these accomplishments China remained a poor country. Population growth absorbed much of the expansion in production and kept pressure on housing stock and other basic elements of the people's livelihoods.

The questions surrounding the appropriate path of socialist construction were complex during these decades. At Liberation China was in rough shape, with much of the economy in a shambles after thirty years of war and revolutionary conflict. Many millions of people were displaced. And the project which lay ahead involved a shift of focus for the party from the countryside to the cities. Building a modern industrialised socialism involved many new challenges beyond the issues of land reform and class transformation in the villages. These concerns also involved theoretical issues of socialism, and these once again were shaped by the dialectic between theory and practice, in sometimes contentious circumstances.

In February 1950, China and the Soviet Union signed a treaty of mutual friendship and assistance. Through the decade of the '50s, Soviet aid to China was critical in getting the process of industrial development underway. Not surprisingly, the Soviet experience of socialist construction had a strong influence on events in China during this period. Yet there were important differences in the material realities of Czarist Russia and Imperial and Republican China which had shaped their respective revolutionary paths. Mao's recognition of large segments of the peasantry as an agricultural proletariat was based on the historical economic structures of China, while the Soviets had dealt with their agricultural sector based on a peasant economy very different from that of China, one without the mode of commercial capitalism which was widespread in the dynastic era.

In the early years of the People's Republic there were significant debates among Marxist historians and economists about the nature of China's historical economy. These may seem somewhat distant from the practical issues of organising production and managing distribution, yet they were critical to understanding the material conditions which underpinned rural life and which inflected the development of the emergent modern industrial sector. As historians investigated China's economy, especially from the Song dynasty (960-1279) on, they found that there were ways in which it had not conformed to the established Marxist orthodoxy of stages of development, from slave society in antiquity to feudalism and then on to capitalism in recent centuries, setting the stage for the transition to socialism. Instead, for more than a thousand years, China had developed its own distinctive forms of production and circulation, a massive economy of commodity production, capital valorisation and accumulation, fully monetised and integrated in market networks spanning the empire, and feeding into far-flung links of global trade. How was this to be understood?

The theoretical model of stages of history had been derived from some comments Marx had made in writing about the specific history of Europe, and especially Britain. These had come to be seen by many as a more universal pattern, and this view was made official by Stalin in the 1930s. The close links between China and the Soviets in the 1950s meant that this model was a kind of orthodoxy with which Chinese historians had to contend. The evidence of economic growth and of the specific forms this took in imperial China had to fit into the established conceptual framework. This led to much debate and discussion about ideas such as the "sprouts of capitalism," a formulation which sought to accommodate the evidence of commercial capitalist features in the historical economy while refraining from saying China had actually had its own form of capitalism, predating that of Europe. Another theoretical approach built on some scattered statements in Marx's writings about an "Asiatic mode of production." But while this formulation could include the idea of China having been in some way distinct from the historical itinerary of the West, it was based on a conception of China, and Asia more broadly, as having been stagnant and undeveloped, which clearly did not fit the evidence of economic dynamism which was accumulating. These efforts to grasp the real historical experience and conditions of China, while not completely breaking with the Soviet-sponsored interpretation, nonetheless reinforced the need for China to seek a path of socialist construction which was truly adapted to its own material circumstances.

The political struggles of these years, from the Great Leap Forward to the Cultural Revolution and the deaths of Zhou Enlai, Zhu De, and Mao Zedong in 1976, centred around the questions of how China should advance along the socialist path. These were years of experimentation, of advances and retreats, successes and failures, yet the goal remained that of building a socialist future for the Chinese people. At the heart of these issues was the essential question of turning the theoretical concept of a social economy in which the wealth produced by working people would be equitably shared among those who produced it into a practical, functioning system of production and distribution within the existing material conditions of China. This was an unprecedented endeavour, given China's large population and geographically diverse territory and endowment of natural resources. The Soviet model was not suitable to the specific circumstances of China. China's leaders had to find their own way, and this was an immensely challenging enterprise. The conflicting views of the way forward which persisted through this period reflected the difficulty of the work in hand, and the necessity of grasping the nuts and bolts of actually existing conditions.

It was only with the death of Mao Zedong in 1976 that the contention between differing groupings within the Communist Party could finally be resolved, though the party retains a diversity of opinion and a commitment to discussion and debate on the issues of socialist construction. The two years from Mao's death to the emergence of Deng Xiaoping as the leading figure at the end of 1978 were a period of intense political reflection and struggle. China had undergone significant economic development in the first thirty years of the PRC, yet it remained a poor country. An egalitarianism of poverty existed, not a socialism of abundance. The leadership reached a consensus that a new approach was needed, one which would enable the rapid growth of production and allow China to achieve a sufficient level of material prosperity to begin to move to more socialist forms of distribution. In order to do this, they decided to launch a great experiment, not without precedent in the Soviet Union's experience of the New Economic Policies in the early 1920s or some of the policies developed in Yugoslavia and Hungary, to use the mechanisms of the market to drive the growth of the productive economy. This was an audacious, indeed risky, venture. The key to its success would be the leading role of the party. Markets, left to their own devices, would not create an equitable distribution of goods and services. The party would need to oversee the operations of markets and capital to restrain the dangers and abuses that would arise and ensure that, as China achieved a level of moderate prosperity, social wealth would increasingly be allocated to address social needs.

The process of developing policies to pursue the goals of reform reveal a new phase in the process of creating socialism with Chinese characteristics. This can be perhaps most clearly seen in the debates and discussions which took place in the 1980s as questions of the extent and pace of reform, and the degree to which market forces should be regulated, were at the top of the agenda. A series of conferences, meetings with delegations from both Western capitalist countries and from the socialist states of Eastern Europe, and the activities of academic working groups all took place as a wide range of ideas were considered. Not surprisingly, many of the participants who came from American or other Western corporate or academic circles advocated all-out marketisation, often referred to as "shock therapy." Some leaders of the party expressed sympathy with this view, such as Hu Yaobang and especially Zhao Ziyang. These ideas did not, however, prevail. Instead, as Isabella Weber has shown in her study of these debates, drawing on both the modern experiences and theoretical insights of Marxism and Leninism, and China's own traditions of economic thought and the long experience of Chinese dynasties in economic affairs, an approach favouring more incremental reform, recognising the need to evaluate progress and identify and tackle problems along the way, was adopted.

China's historical political economy encompassed a field that, since at least the 10th century, featured a vast and intricate network of markets and specialised areas of production. Some parts of the empire became centres of textile or ceramic production. Others were the regions of primary agricultural output, feeding grain into national market systems to feed areas where households pursued livelihoods not based in farming. The imperial state had long followed policies of market buffering such as maintaining the "Ever Normal Granaries" to hold reserves of rice, wheat, or other grains. The state would purchase grain at harvest time, when prices tended to be low, in order to shore up the market. In times of scarcity, before harvest time or when crops failed, grain could be sold from the reserves to keep prices within reach of hungry people. The state also operated monopolies in certain critical commodities such as salt. On the one hand these served as sources of revenue for the state, but they also functioned to prevent profiteering in goods that were deemed essential to people's basic needs.

Beyond these state policies China also had a rich literature of economic thought. Some of this came from classical antiquity, such as the writings of Guanzi, or the Han dynasty's "Debates on Salt and Iron", which set out the arguments for and against state intervention in the economy. As China's economy became one with a large portion of commercial capitalism from the 10th century on, writers of the Song, Ming, and Qing dynasties elaborated their ideas about the management of wealth, the proper relationship between the state and the economy, and the impact of markets on social and cultural life, as well as publishing descriptions of productive processes and discussions of technological innovations. This reservoir of economic knowledge was explicitly drawn upon in the economic debates of the 1980s, in a very concrete effort to shape China's socialist path through a dialectical dynamic of past and present as well as local and global conditions.

At the end of the 1980s, social contradictions which had emerged in response to some aspects of reform, especially the ill-considered price reforms of 1988 and the growth of corruption, gave rise to protests in Beijing and other cities. Sadly, what began as an expression of concern about the pace of reform and its impact on certain urban groupings like professionals and educated young people, came to be hijacked by radical anti-government elements, overtly and covertly supported and assisted by foreign interests. The occupation of central Beijing, the nation's capital, which seriously disrupted both government functions and the normal life of the city, persisted for six weeks. In the end order had to be restored, though this was not done without serious deliberation and as a last resort. A period of international criticism and a certain degree of isolation for China ensued, as well as a period of careful reflection and assessment of the path forward. Renewed debates about the reform process took place, which culminated in a determination to stay the course and carry through the work of socialist construction.

Deng Xiaoping made an inspection tour of southern China in 1992, during which he made a number of statements about the need to revive and reinvigorate the policies of reform and opening to the outside. It was at this point, too, that Deng emphasised, in his discussions with other leaders, the idea that China needed to "bide our time and develop our capabilities." In order for the reform project to succeed, and for the Chinese people to achieve an early stage of socialism, namely a moderately prosperous society, the economy needed to grow, and to achieve this China needed access to the financial, technological, and intellectual resources of the global capitalist system. Investment by foreign corporations would bring new productive capacities to China, and would also stimulate domestic development. In order to achieve these objectives, Deng argued, it was necessary to 'go along to get along' with the West, especially the United States. So China should keep a low profile in terms of its efforts to build a socialist future. This led to the era when Chinese leaders talked about China's "peaceful rise" and the need for a "harmonious society." This period of accommodation with global capitalism extended through the 1990s and well into the first decade of the twenty-first century. China joined the World Trade Organisation, took part in a wide variety of international organisations, and cooperated with the United States in a number of areas.

The era of accommodation encouraged political elites in America, and in many cases academics and even some on the left, to believe that China was on a path leading to political transformation, and that the country would abandon its socialist project and become a subordinate component of the world capitalist system. This fantasy served the political interests of the American ruling class, as they dreamed of regime change and the profits to be reaped from an ever more compliant China. It was in these years that the belief spread among many on the left that China had indeed taken the capitalist road, and had become just another great power. Liberals, progressives, and even Marxists who otherwise opposed American imperialism now spoke of "a pox on both their houses," seeing China as "just as bad" as America. This was a serious misreading by both the elites and these former friends of China.

In 2008, financial speculation and other reckless ventures in pursuit of ever greater profits for the already super rich caused Western capitalist economies to go into freefall. Banks and other investment corporations collapsed, millions of people lost their homes, and millions more suffered severe financial hardship. Consumer demand evaporated as households in the US and the rest of the capitalist core saw their incomes fall and their savings disappear. This had a drastic impact on China. Around twenty million Chinese working in factories producing goods for export to the West were laid off as demand collapsed. This was a severe crisis, not of China's making. How the Communist Party and the government of the People's Republic managed this crisis demonstrated the real nature of China's socialist system.

In the US and the rest of the capitalist world, workers laid off from their jobs faced futures of great precarity. Available unemployment benefits were minimal and lasted only for short periods of time. As the financial crisis deepened and persisted, more and more families lost their homes, faced difficulties in feeding their children, and many became homeless. Parks and other open spaces in and around American cities filled up with desperate people living in tents or other jerry-built shelter, while the capitalist speculators who had brought about the crisis were bailed out by Congress with taxpayer money, and rewarded themselves with giant bonuses from those federal funds.

In China, as part of the socialist legal and institutional infrastructure, all citizens have a household registration, which entitles them to basic social services like housing, health care, education, and other necessities. Most of the workers laid off in 2008 came from villages in the interior, while they worked in cities along the coast. They were able to return to the villages and were eligible there for the basic support of these state programs. This doesn't mean they were living lives of luxury. Basic support is just that, basic. But they were not cast out on the street, left to their own devices. As the government worked to redirect investment towards more domestic consumption and less reliance on exports, people were taken care of in their home communities. As the demand for labour recovered with new investment by the state, these workers could either return to their previous jobs or find new ones. In a year or so the crisis had passed, without the terrible suffering endured by Americans and others in the West. This clearly demonstrated the strength of China's socialist system.

It was also, however, something of a wake-up for the capitalist elites in the US. The illusion of a future in which China would "change colour" and become a compliant subordinate in the global capitalist system was shown to be just that, a false hope. Along with other political factors such as the winding down of the imperialist "war on terror", this led to a major shift in American policy towards China. In November 2011 the Obama administration announced a 'pivot to Asia," a redeployment of American military assets to escalate the longstanding campaign of encircling China. Secretary of State Hilary Clinton wrote an article in Foreign Affairs calling for a "new American Pacific Century." China was now targeted as a rising power in the world which challenged American global hegemony. China's rise, especially as a socialist alternative to imperialist domination, had to be stopped.

In this context, the election of Xi Jinping in 2012, and the "new era" which has come to be associated with his leadership, can be seen as both the logical next, third phase in the history of the People's Republic, and as a response to the new posture of hostility towards China adopted by the U.S. and its subordinate allies. When the reform policies were first launched at the end of the 1970s and beginning of the '80s it was understood by the leadership that the use of market mechanisms would generate contradictions, such as corruption, inequality, and environmental stresses. It was imperative that the Communist Party maintain its leading role in order to contain and control the adverse consequences of rapid economic growth and development. It was necessary to adopt a low profile for the socialist agenda while the initial period of expansion was underway. But as China achieved the level of moderate prosperity in the first years of the twenty-first century, it became possible to use socially accumulated wealth to begin to address the contradictions which had emerged.

Xi Jinping has led the implementation of new initiatives to do just this. A major anti-corruption campaign began and continues. Efforts to address environmental concerns have been a top priority, with China becoming a global leader in alternative energy, electric vehicles, and other areas. A massive targeted anti-poverty campaign has a hundred people to a higher material quality of life. Healthcare, education, and other social services have been significantly expanded. China has become more self-confident and more assertive in international affairs, no longer feeling the need to accommodate itself to American imperialism. There has been a renewed emphasis on Marxism in public discourse, and a commitment to fulfil the original mission of the revolution, to improve the lives of the Chinese people through building a socialist future for the country.

China has not yet reached the goal of a fully developed socialism. Much work remains to be done. Real challenges and risks continue to be faced. What can be seen clearly, however, is that the task of adapting the insights and analytical methodology of Marxism to the actually existing, and continually developing conditions of China has been the key to the process of creating socialism with Chinese characteristics. The future of this dialectical project will require dedication, innovation, and the power of revolutionary optimism. The flag stays red, and the struggle continues.

THIS PAGE INTENTIONALLY LEFT BLANK

2

China's transition to socialism: 1949-1956

Jenny Clegg

INTRODUCTION

OCTOBER 1st 1949 – a day that shook China and shook the world. From the rostrum in Tiananmen Square, Mao declares victory for the Chinese revolution. The atmosphere is euphoric. The people's war is won and the Chinese people have stood up. A new China is born.

Mao's speech was to resonate across time, back over a century of squalor and impoverishment, foreign humiliation and war, and forward to today as China steps with confidence onto the world stage.

The establishment of the People's Republic of China (PRC) was the culmination of decades of struggle against the imperialist powers and their proxies, the four big 'bureaucrat capitalist' families and their supporters. After 12 consecutive years of war, and a century of imperialist subjugation, now was the chance for peace so long yearned for by the Chinese people. Now was the chance to end the system of land monopoly that had condemned the peasants to a seemingly endless struggle for survival on tiny parcels of land, their lives punctuated by famine and flood.

The people's victory offered inspiration for oppressed nations and peoples struggling for liberation around the world, just as it sent the US into a frenzy over "who lost China?"

China was now to enter the final stage of New Democracy ready to pave the way for socialist transition. Understanding the years from 1949 to 1956 is essential to appreciating the meaning of China today. This period was to see the creation of political conditions for the foundation of a new socialist state – the formation of a government to serve the people, addressing the need to feed and clothe the population of 500 million, the vast majority impoverished farmers – whilst taking the first steps towards industrialisation and modernisation as it built up the base of state ownership in industry and collective ownership in the rural economy.

Rehabilitation: 1949-1953

The challenges ahead were immense. In the eight years of anti-Japanese resistance and three years of civil war, China had seen over 40 million people killed or wounded, and some 100 million, almost 20 percent of the population, condemned to years of aimless migration. Under Kuomintang/ Guomindang (KMT) rule, corruption and hyper-inflation had become rampant.

A Chinese People's Political Consultative Conference under the leadership of the Communist Party of China (CPC), including representatives from the eight democratic parties, was quickly set up to agree a common programme for China's recovery. However, apart from governing a number of liberated areas mainly in the North and North West for a few years, the CPC had little experience of urban conditions or of industry.

That it took just three years to rehabilitate the society and economy overall is truly remarkable: we might think of Sudan or Haiti or Myanmar today to appreciate this. Although the contexts are very different, nevertheless the experience of humanitarian catastrophe is universal.

By 1953, the People's Liberation Army (PLA) had pacified the entire country, clearing the countryside of endemic banditry as well as the remnant KMT reactionary forces; Tibet was liberated peacefully and the entire mainland unified. Foreign owned or comprador capital as well as Japanese enterprises taken over by the KMT were confiscated, creating a state owned industrial core alongside a private capitalist sector. Land reform spread from North to South completing the redistribution of 44 percent of the land, from the landlords – roughly four percent of the population – to the poor and middle peasants, roughly 80 percent of the population. Rich and well-to-do peasants retained their holdings, their surpluses keeping the cities fed.

With control over finance, credit and commerce in its hands, the new government set about bringing down inflation, and stabilising prices and taxation. Factories were restarted and the economy brought back into growth. Programmes were launched to repair public works, and rehabilitate the beggars, prostitutes and petty criminals that had swarmed the streets.

The year 1951 saw the launch of city-based mass campaigns: the Three Antis – corruption, waste and bureaucratism – was targeted at government and Party officials and state-owned enterprise managers, whilst the Five Antis campaign against tax evasion, theft of state property, cheating on labour and materials and stealing state economic intelligence was directed at the capitalist class.

Transformative democratic legislation was passed: the Marriage Law of 1950 abolished the feudal patriarchal system of concubinage, child betrothal and coerced marriage, introducing free choice marriage, and with this the establishment of equal rights for men and women. Arrangements for regional autonomy in 1953 established equal rights for China's 55 national minorities, at that time comprising six percent of the population, legislating freedom to develop their own languages and to preserve or reform their traditions and religious beliefs.

All this was achieved in the face of extreme hostility from the US which imposed a total embargo when China entered the Korean war in 1950, one even tougher than that applied to the USSR.[1] The war was also a massive drain on resources and manpower, but by 1953 the Chinese volunteers had brought the advance of the US-led forces to a standstill.

Some one million KMT officials had fled to Taiwan and elsewhere overseas, leaving a huge skills gap in the administration, compounding the problem of the inexperience of the CPC cadres. To have accomplished so much in such a short space of time required novel methods.

Joshua Horn, a British surgeon who volunteered to work in China in 1954 was to discover the importance of meetings in the life of the hospital staff.

> Some were confined to a single ward, some involved everyone in the hospital, from the directors to the laundry workers. We sometimes discussed local matters such as why an operation had failed to achieve the expected result… how a complaint of a patient should be dealt with… how we could improve the efficiency of the outpatient department… Sometimes we discussed national or international questions such as why agriculture should be taken as the foundation of the national economy and industry the leading factor… whether we were satisfied with our Trade Union, why the Chinese government aided emerging countries.[2]

These meetings, big and small, were, he recognised, key to a high degree of working efficiency, with 'correct decisions [being made] on the basis of unity of purpose' with everyone understanding and supporting these decisions'.

Participatory methods helped to fill the skills gap and reorientate the two million or so KMT officials who remained and had been left in post. The Three Antis and the Five Antis mass movements were a training ground for new leaders as the United Front parties and professional bodies, together with the labour, youth, and women's organisations, helped to extend campaigns across the urban population. Land reform also brought forward millions of village level cadres to take the place of the traditional rural elites. Villagers participated in meetings to assign every family a class status so as to decide on the distribution of landlords' land to land-short middle and poor peasants.

From New Democracy to socialism 1953-1956

By 1953, the PRC was ready to turn its focus to the tasks of industrialisation and socialist transition, transforming the mixed economy into a system of public ownership and laying the Soviet-style institutional foundations of Five Year Plans (FYPs) along with a National People's Congress (NPC) based on People's Congresses down to township levels.

As people had seen inflation fall, taxation stabilise and the ethos of plain living and hard work replace the extravagance and waste of the former officials, their confidence in the new government as capable of acting in their interests was growing; the next step was to win the vast majority to socialism.

The first constitution, ratified by the NPC in 1954, designated the PRC a 'people's democratic state led by the working class, based on the worker-peasant alliance'. The socialisation of ownership was to take place over a fairly long period of three FYPs: the policy was to protect the capitalists' right to own means of production and to 'use, restrict and transform capitalist industry', transforming it into a system of ownership by the whole people through 'administrative control, leadership by the state sector and supervision by the workers'. In agriculture, the rich peasant economy was to be restricted and ultimately replaced by the organisation of individual peasant households into cooperatives.[3]

Such modern industries as China possessed were fragmented across clusters around Shanghai, inland in Wuhan and the North East. This latter had come under threat during the Korean war, exposing the extreme vulnerability of the Chinese economy. Handicrafts were also widespread, forming a large sector of the economy.

The emphasis of the first FYP, following Soviet lines, was on heavy industry, with the coordinated and dispersed development of 156 large scale capital intensive projects greatly expanding state ownership. These were to be funded by loans from the Soviet Union and took up half of industrial investment for the period. Given China's lack of expertise, the Soviet Union sent 10,000 experts, with 28,000 Chinese going to the USSR for training in what must be one of the largest transfers of technology in history.[4]

Meanwhile private companies, which accounted for nearly 50 percent of industrial output in 1949,[5] were to be steadily shifted into joint arrangements with the state under the dual pressures of discriminatory taxes and workers' committees tasked to clamp down on graft and ensure integration into the state-run marketing system.

In the rural areas, cooperation was to proceed step by step from the formation of Mutual Aid teams, joining together the labour, tools and draught animals of a few families, to elementary Agricultural Producers Cooperatives (APCs) of some 20 to 40 households organising joint farming, to advanced APCs of 100 to 200 households which were regarded as fully socialist in bringing all means of production – tools and land – under collective village ownership and management.

Driving the process were the poorer peasants – 60 to 70 percent of the rural population – who, despite benefitting from land reform, still lived on the borderline of subsistence. A new polarisation between rich and poor was emerging as individual farmers, lacking tools and draught animals, risked bankruptcy, forcing them to sell up to the more well-to-do and resort to hiring out their labour. Cooperation offered the solution to their problems, pooling all available resources for the benefit of the village as a whole.

1956: The Socialist Victory

A speech by Mao in July 1955 calling for a 'socialist upsurge' to accelerate the speed of rural cooperative development was to bring forward the socialist transition by ten years.[6] By October 1955, a total of 32 percent of households were in APCs; then within eight months by June 1956 virtually the entire countryside – 90 percent of households – had joined the system, nearly two thirds of them members of the advanced, fully socialist organisations.[7]

By this time capitalist industry had also been more or less completely amalgamated under large-scale joint state-private or state-owned operations, its share of output falling to 13 percent in 1955 and then to zero within the year.[8] 90 percent of individual handicrafts people were also joined in cooperatives.

By 1956, Communist Party membership had grown from 2.7 million 1947 to 10.7 million, nearly 70 percent peasants; trade union organisations numbered 12 million members; and the China New Democratic Youth League, renamed the Communist Youth League, had a membership of 20 million.[9] With this mass base of support for socialism, in September 1956, the Eighth CPC Congress was to declare a 'total and decisive' victory for China's socialist transformation.

The fact that the national bourgeoisie 'heralded its acceptance… with a fanfare of gongs and drums', was, the Congress noted, 'something of a miracle'.[10] This was seen to determine a period of long-term co-existence between the CPC and the democratic parties representing the national bourgeoisie and intelligentsia. Accepting these classes as part of the working people after the socialist transition, China's state power was considered in essence to have become 'a form of dictatorship of the proletariat'.[11]

This speedy transition was assisted by an impressive social and economic record with faster growth in both the producer and consumer goods sectors between 1949 to 1956 together with considerable improvements in the living conditions of the people. Land redistribution had reduced inequalities; living standards had risen by nearly 20 percent from 1936; life expectancy rose to 45 from perhaps as low as 25 in the 1930s, with a significant fall of 40 percent in mortality levels.[12] This was due not just to the end of war but also reductions in infant mortality with improvements in nutritional levels for the rural poor as well as the promotion of preventive medicine, the training of midwives and successful public health campaigns.

From its base of socialist ownership within modern industry, banking and commerce, the state utilised its position to manage the class alliances, allowing anti-capitalist struggles to develop peacefully through calibrated popular mobilisations.

As Mao was to explain in 1955, the reason why the CPC chose to maintain its alliance with the national bourgeoisie, refraining for the time being from confiscating capitalist enterprises, was to secure manufactured goods to meet the needs of the peasants and overcome their reluctance to sell their produce – grain and industrial raw materials. At the same time, the alliance with the peasants allowed the state to secure grain and industrial materials with which to bring the bourgeoisie under control, since to get raw materials they had to sell manufactured goods to the state, entering into closer integration into the state ownership system.[13]

Underpinning state policies were worker and peasant mobilisations, interacting one with the another. As the advance of agrarian reform after 1949 brought the peasants on side, this in turn helped stimulate the anti-corruption movements in the cities, imposing restrictions on government officials and capitalist enterprises.

After 1953, restrictions on the rich peasant economy were increasingly tightened through progressive taxation with low interest loans from credit cooperatives undercutting opportunities for moneylending, whilst the supply and marketing cooperatives' control of prices limited possibilities for market speculation. Then as poor peasants sought their own solutions via mutual aid and cooperation, the rich peasants were also deprived of hired labour.[14]

As the opportunities for individual enrichment were cut off, the well-to-do farmers were incentivised to join the APCs with offers of compensation for pooling their draught animals and farm tools. This was to finally end the basis of rural capitalism – the buying and selling of land.

Of the two key alliances, the alliance with the peasants was fundamental.

The final elimination of capitalism in the countryside, Mao considered, would isolate the bourgeoisie politically and block the capitalist road of free markets that they wanted to follow.[15] As pressures applied by the state above and the workers' committees below hastened the integration of private enterprises into the socialist economy. At the same time nationalisation was eased by compensation as fixed interest was to continue to be paid to owners who were generally kept on as managers.

By this mixture of restrictions and incentives the transition to socialism was to be accomplished peacefully.

Breaking through the Soviet orthodoxy

In his July 1955 speech, Mao was to criticise those advocating caution for 'tottering along like a woman with bound feet.'[16] If there was a certain wariness against 'rash advance' amongst other leaders, no doubt conscious of Soviet experience of collectivisation, Mao sensed the time was right for bold advance with political conditions changing in the villages.

With new inequalities emerging, restrictions on private gain were proving popular, isolating the rich peasants, whilst the local cadres, seeing the support for cooperation broadening, and becoming more experienced themselves, were growing more confident. 'We must protect the enthusiasm of the cadres and masses and not pour cold water on them,' Mao was to insist.[17] If the moment was lost, and poor peasant farms allowed to go under, labour hiring would grow and the rich peasant economy would become established.

In the event, the rate of cooperation exceeded even Mao's expectations. Despite the speed, change was generally peaceful, avoiding serious losses in agricultural production very much in contrast to the Soviet experience.[18]

The CPC at this time was also in intense debate over whether mechanisation should precede collectivisation or vice versa. Mechanisation was recognised as essential to increasing farm productivity in support of industrialisation without sacrificing food security, and tractors and other modern inputs offered the peasants tangible benefits to participating in collectivisation voluntarily. But this meant prioritising accumulation over consumption to speed the development of heavy industry.

It was not so much that this Soviet approach was considered wrong but that it was too costly: as Mao said, 'it squeezed the peasants too hard'.[19] Russia at the time of the October Revolution had had a more advanced industrial base; in China the countryside was preponderant in the economy. Soviet planners had sought to speed the flow of resources from agriculture to build up industry but this centralised approach was not feasible in China given its low surplus and extreme poverty. Unlike the Bolsheviks who had to win peasant support after the seizure of power, China's revolution had been made by the peasants – it could not afford to wait 10 years for industrial capacity to develop to meet peasant demands; it was imperative that both grain and cotton production were increased.

Underlying Mao's emphasis on politics was a certain economic logic. China's rice-based agriculture had much room to increase output through labour intensive land reclamation, small scale irrigation and water conservation works, double cropping and other improvements in cultivation. At the same time poor peasant labour was under-utilised especially during the slack winter months.

Rather than prioritising capital intensive mechanisation, Mao's strategy was to collectivise first and accumulate capital to support industrialisation by increasing agricultural output on the basis of available resources. Using little or no capital investment, cooperatives could exploit economies of scale, amalgamating tiny plots cultivated by individual households, as well as mobilise the peasants in labour intensive improvements, and in addition pool savings to purchase more means of production whilst also establishing welfare funds for the sick and elderly.

The experience of the socialist upsurge saw Mao break with Soviet socialist orthodoxy, his emphasis on class relations and the worker-peasant alliance in particular contrasting with the Soviet economists who tended to view the relationship between industry and agriculture in terms of the 'price scissors'.[20]

For Mao, planning was not just a technocratic or bureaucratic exercise. In his 1956 essay *On the Ten Major Relationships*, he takes China's development as an interconnected whole, identifying linkages not only in the economic, but also in the political and social structures key to shaping future directions.

A year later, in *On the Correct Handling of Contradictions Among the People* he noted that given the ongoing influence of Western educated intellectuals, ideological struggle between capitalism and socialism would continue over a fairly long period of time. At the same time he pointed out that even antagonistic contradictions could be handled in non-antagonistic ways, or even transformed into non-antagonistic ones, as indeed the peaceful transition from New Democracy to socialism had shown.

Beyond 1956: Travelling without a map

Mao's two essays, drawn from the lessons of the transition, opened up new directions for socialist China. The task ahead was to put them into practice; the challenges going forward were massive.

After 1953, planners had veered between stabilisation and popular mobilisation as they struggled to handle the contradictions between consumption and investment for rapid growth. These zig-zags were to become even more exaggerated after 1956: a more cautious second FYP was derailed after two years by the Great Leap Forward (GLF), the 3rd then delayed by three years. Between 1965 and 1975, the NPC and the CPPCC, in which the non-Communist parties participated, ceased to function.

The failure of the state to respond effectively in the years of famine from 1959 to 1962 brought out in terrible relief flaws in central-local government links,[21] then later efforts in the Cultural Revolution to 'revolutionise the superstructure' descended into factionalism and anarchy. At the same time China's problems were compounded as it neglected population planning: with mortality rates falling, although grain production rose, there were ever more mouths to feed.

In a major speech in 2021 assessing the historical experience of the CPC over the past century, Xi Jinping deemed that 'a completely erroneous appraisal of the prevailing class relations and the political situation in the Party and the country' had been made in this period.[22] Circumstances however had become ever more challenging.

The international situation which in 1956 was seen to be favourable to China's socialist construction, was beginning to worsen. In the mid-1950s, socialism had spread across Eastern Europe and in Asia and national resistance against imperialism had been rising. The year 1954 saw the PRC's premier and foreign affairs minister, Zhou Enlai, make a breakthrough agreement with Indian Prime Minister Nehru on the Five Principles of Peaceful Coexistence which the following year were incorporated into the principles adopted at the Afro–Asian Conference in Bandung.

However, with the US expanding its imperialist reach, setting up new bases, it was clear it was preparing for war. In 1958, the US deployed nuclear weapons around Taiwan.[23] Meanwhile strains in Sino-Soviet relations, following Khrushchev's secret speech denouncing Stalin at the 20th Congress of the CPSU, were growing. The need to bolster military capacity as external circumstances demanded placed ever greater pressure on the limited surpluses.

The socialist future after 1956 also called for education, healthcare, science and culture – the new media of film and radio broadcasting – all to be geared to the needs of the rural population, who despite improvements, were still largely illiterate and exposed to disease. The inbuilt urban bias of services threatened to alienate their support, as did the growing bureaucracy, costly as it was and permeated by the elitist traditions of the Confucian scholar-official and the disdain for manual labour.

The domestic situation became more and more radicalised with the international shift to people's war propelled by Vietnam's determined resistance to the US brutal occupation of its Southern part. As US aggression spilled over into Laos, serried ranks of Red Guards sent out a warning against extending the war to China. After the youth were dispatched to the countryside, not least to ease the strain on resources, the Cultural Revolution search for a new socialist superstructure entangled itself in confusion over the nature of the state.[24]

Returning to 1956 foundations

The change again in the international situation – with the improved relations between the US and China from the early 1970s, and in particular the establishment of bilateral relations on 1 January 1979 – created space for Deng's 'reform and opening up' which in a way took up where the 8th Party Congress in 1956 left off. China was soon to return to its original socialist foundations – the five year plans, formulated now more as flexible guidelines than bureaucratic targets, together with the United Front government of the NPC and the CPPCC under CPC leadership.

It did so though at a higher level: the later Mao era should not be entirely written off. It saw the building up of a comprehensive industrial base whilst peoples' basic needs in food and clothing were essentially met; knowledge and improved agricultural techniques were disseminated throughout the countryside; rural health had improved through the barefoot doctors' scheme; and overall life expectancy rose to 64 in 1975;[25] the role and place of women had been transformed; and rural industries, from which peasants were to see the benefits, spread across the countryside, subsequently taking off under reform policies in the 1990s and early 2000s, contributing to much of the rapid economic growth.

Nor was the return to individual farming to reverse the achievements of the socialist upsurge: village collective ownership of the land has served now for decades as a basic safety net for farmers in a marketised environment whilst cooperatives of various types – supply and marketing, credit, handicraft, specialist cooperatives of fruit and vegetable producers and so on – continue to shape the way the rural economy develops.

Conclusion

October 1949 marked a turning point for China and for the world. The path was cleared for socialism, with China embarking on an entirely new course of relations with Africa and Asia, the first steps in the remaking the international order.

Of necessity, a general outline leaves out the detail of mistakes and flaws, but overall it cannot be doubted that this transformation was brought about with massive popular support. In the end it was the upsurge of the cooperative movement – the outcome of years of revolutionary change in the rural areas – that lifted the worker-peasant alliance to a new level carrying China into the socialist stage.

This was a transformation driven not just by ideological fervour or alternatively coercion, as sometimes portrayed in the West. Voluntary change was to be accomplished through a combination of Soviet-style state policy and the CPC's own participative style of consensual management and flexible methods of trial and error.

A careful handling of class relations allowed the peoples' struggles against capitalism to unfold in sequenced steps, workers and peasants discussing and educating themselves as they engaged in policy implementation. Grassroots cadres, learning on the job, built broad support as the dynamics of class struggle exposed the inherent contradictions at each step. Popular mobilisations pushed against bureaucratic inertia, making bold advances which kept opposition on the back foot.

By equating socialism with prosperity, grassroots cadres were able to appeal to peasant self-interest, fusing theory with practice. As the British academic Vivienne Shue spells out:

the mass line meant precisely to take the practical concerns of the mass of the peasants... and find solutions for them in terms of the theory of revolution.[26]

The success of the upsurge in the countryside created a new foundation for the socialist economy in support of industrialisation as key to development. There was still a long way to go: it was to take many more decades, and huge challenges to be faced and overcome, before the PRC was to eliminate extreme poverty. But it was the particularly flexible combination of ideology and pragmatism which enabled the country's leaders to break through Soviet orthodoxy, ultimately allowing the PRC to find its own way forward, not without pain, in pursuit of 'socialism with Chinese characteristics'.

NOTES

1. Michael Yahuda. *The International Politics of the Asia-Pacific*. 3rd ed. London and New York: Routledge, 2011, p99
2. Joshua Horn. *Away With All Pests*. New York and London: Monthly Review Press, 1969, pp30-31
3. *Constitution of the Peoples Republic of China* (1954), accessed 6 June 2024, http://www.lawinfochina.com/display.aspx?lib=law&id=14754&CGid
4. John King Fairbank, *The Great Chinese Revolution 1800-1985*. London: Picador, 1986, p285; Chris Bramall. *Chinese Economic Development*. London and New York: Routledge, 2009, p99
5. Bramall, *ibid*, p90, Table 3.1
6. Mao Zedong. 'On the Cooperative Transformation of Agriculture'. *Selected Works*, Vol. V. Beijing: Foreign Languages Press, 1977
7. Vivienne Shue. *Peasant China in Transition: the Dynamics of Development towards Socialism, 1949-1956*. Los Angeles and London: University of California Press, 1980, pp286-7
8. Bramall, *op cit*, p90, Table 3.1
9. Liu Shaoqi. *Political Report of the CC.CPC to the Eighth National Congress of the CPC*, Marxist Internet Archive, accessed 6 June 2024, https://www.marxists.org/subject/china/documents/cpc/8th_congress.htm
10. *ibid*
11. *ibid*
12. Bramall, *op cit*, p104.
13. Mao Zedong. 1955. 'The Debate on the Co-operative Transformation of Agriculture and the Current Class Struggle'. *Selected Works*, Vol. V. Beijing: Foreign Languages Press, 1977, pp213-214
14. Shue, *op cit*, pp276-7
15. Mao Zedong. 1955. 'The Debate on the Co-operative Transformation of Agriculture and the Current Class Struggle'. *Selected Works*, Vol. V. Beijing: Foreign Languages Press, 1977, p214
16. Mao Zedong. 1955. 'On the Cooperative Transformation of Agriculture'. *Selected Works*, Vol. V. Beijing: Foreign Languages Press, 1977, p184
17. Mao Zedong. 1956. 'Speech at the Second Plenary Session of the Eighth CC CPC' *Selected Works*, Vol. V. Beijing: Foreign Languages Press, 1977, p334
18. Shue, *op cit*, notes China's rapid transition to socialism in the countryside was accomplished with minimal violence and disorder and without a disastrous drop in agricultural output. p2
19. Mao Zedong. 1956. 'On the Ten Major Relationships'. *Selected Works*, Vol. V. Beijing: Foreign Languages Press, 1977, p291

20 The term 'price scissors' describes the tendency for prices of manufactured goods to rise relative to the price of agricultural goods, making it more expensive for peasants to purchase consumer goods and agricultural means of production.

21 Poor weather conditions were an important causal factor of the famine. At the same time, the attention of the CPC leadership was drawn away from domestic matters to the deteriorating relationship with the USSR as Khrushchev openly criticised China's people's communes whilst attempting to improve Soviet relations with the US.

22 Xi Jinping. 2021. 'Explanation of the *Resolution of the CC CPC on the Major Achievements and Historical Experience of the Party over the Past Century*', Xinhuanet, accessed 6 June 2024, http://www.news.cn/english/2021-11/16/c_1310314613.htm

23 This followed an earlier deployment by the US of nuclear-capable of aircraft carriers in 1954. Joseph Gerson. *Empire and the Bomb*. London: Pluto Press, 2007, pp84-89

24 This was reflected in a short succession of changes in the PRC constitution in 1975, 1978 and 1982. The 1975 Constitution changed the 1954 designation of a 'people's democratic state' to that of a 'dictatorship of the proletariat'. *The Constitution of the People's Republic of China*, Beijing: Foreign Languages Press, 1975, Article 1. This was retained in 1978. The matter was finally resolved in 1982 in a new constitution which established the People's Republic of China as a socialist state under the people's democratic dictatorship. This has remained the position to this day. npc.gov.cn. accessed 20 June 2024, http://www.npc.gov.cn/zgrdw/englishnpc/Constitution/node_2825.htm

25 World Bank. accessed 20 June 2024, https://data.worldbank.org/indicator/SP.DYN.LE00.IN?locations=CN

26 Shue, *op cit*, pp333-5

THIS PAGE INTENTIONALLY LEFT BLANK

3

Standing up, living long, opposing hegemony

Andrew Murray

There is a story, possibly apocryphal, regarding a parliamentary by-election in St Pancras, north London, in 1949. The Communist Party stood a candidate and, amidst a deteriorating Cold War atmosphere, polled fairly dismally.

Johnnie Campbell, a laconic Scotsman central to the CPGB's leadership for decades, was dispatched to the locality to rally the troops in the aftermath. Surveying his dispirited comrades, he supposedly declared: "Well, things aren't going our way in St Pancras right now... but we've won in China!"[1]

To many, that was the immediate significance of the Chinese Revolution. For millions of Communists and sympathisers around the world, as well as oppressed masses in the colonies and semi-colonies, the victory of the Communist Party of China (CPC) and the party-led People's Liberation Army was a huge advance – really the greatest conceivable – in a worldwide process of socialist revolution.

Stalin himself, sitting at the centre of that process, believed that victory in China, however cautiously he approached the issue for several years (something he later conceded was probably a mistake, and he did not admit to many), would make the triumph of the Communist cause certain.

And this perception was not an aberration. It was mirrored in the USA by a ruling class that found the new regime in China an almost existential menace, triggering a debate as to who in Washington had "lost China", as if it was naturally US property to mislay.

That was one evaluation, in its own time, of the significance of the Chinese Revolution. Perhaps it seems archaic today. That may speak to the wisdom attributed to Zhou Enlai in 1971, almost certainly apocryphally in this case, that it was too early to judge the impact of the French Revolution (he was likely actually referring, more reasonably, to *les evenements* of May 1968).

Nevertheless, the historical significance of great events is not a static measure. Like a sub-atomic particle, it can apparently be in several places at once, and the point of observation is critical. For example, the historical weight of the October Revolution appears different after 1991 than it did before – to extend the metaphor perhaps beyond reasonable utility, it has shifted from shining star to background radiation.

So any judgement on the significance of the great revolution in China on its 75th anniversary is provisional. 75 years is not so very long. We would speak of it as roughly a single lifetime and there is one gauge straight away. The citizen born in China today can expect to live three years longer, to the age of 78. In 1949, they would not have expected to live beyond the age of 40.

There is the significance in a single statistic, probably the most important of all. "Live long and prosper" as Mr Spock enjoined in *Star Trek* and People's China has made good on that Vulcan salutation. More than a billion people are living longer and prospering as never before.

One could stop there, considering enough said. But that would pause our inquiry at the surface of things, like describing the ruins of an earthquake without a nod at the movement of tectonic plates.

Perhaps the significance of the People's Republic of China (PRC) proceeds along three distinct but closely entwined axes.

The first is the "standing up" of China itself, its transformation from the mutilated prey of sundry imperialisms and a laggard in world standards of social development, into a mighty power in sight of having the world's largest national economy. This reverses what has been called the 'great divergence' in economic power and prosperity, which began with the 19th-century opium wars imposed on China by the British and opened up an enormous gap in favour of the west over succeeding decades. The extension of life expectancy in China is only the most dramatic manifestation of this transformation. This is the developmental axis.

Second, it both represents and further encourages a global shift of power from the West European/North American bloc which hegemonised two centuries of history towards what we now call the Global South. It challenges the monopoly of global violence at the state level exercised by the United States and its allies. This is the democratic and, however much today's CPC might be reluctant to embrace the term, actually anti-imperialist axis.

Third, by maintaining a socialist orientation after other developments in that direction have faltered, it both keeps open the possibility of plural systemic options in the world, frustrating Washington dreams of ideological unipolarity, and prevents socialism itself from being pushed into the shadows of history, even as it reconceptualises what socialism might mean. That is the socialist axis, and it may be the most contested on the left.

Let us look at each a little more closely, if briefly, acknowledging that so interconnected are these axes that any delineation between them is somewhat arbitrary and points made under one heading could just as well, with some reformulation, be developed under another.

China Stands Up

Charles Beresford was a pillar of 19th century Empire, remembered mainly for his role in the Royal Navy (*inter alia* he took part in the bombardment of Alexandria in the interests of British bondholders in 1882 and later participated in the failed relief of General Gordon at Khartoum). Doubtless bored while serving as MP for York at the turn of the century in a hiatus in his naval obligations, he was engaged by the Associated Chambers of Commerce to travel to China. His mission was to establish what might be the best conditions to ensure the security of British investments there at a time when Britain accounted for nearly two-thirds of China's total foreign trade.

A moot point was whether the British government should push for an "open door" policy, under which all of the Chinese Empire would be opened to plunder by all imperialists alike, or whether it should promote a division into spheres of influence – British, French, Japanese, German and so on. Upon his return Lord Beresford wrote a book setting out his findings. It is called, simply enough, *The Break-Up of China*.[2]

In this work, he reproduces a memorandum submitted to him during his visit by the Chairman of the China Association at Shanghai, one C.J. Dudgeon, representing the views of British capitalist interests in that great metropolis. Once he had got past a litany of complaints concerning conditions in China, Mr Dudgeon suggested remedy:

> The necessitous financial condition of China, brought about by the disaster of her war with Japan, and her obligations thereby incurred with European countries, makes it plain that a continuation of her policy of exclusion, and contempt for foreign ways, cannot longer be maintained. *Pressure from without, powerfully aided by an empty exchequer within* [emphasis added], has already persuaded her rulers that the vast natural resources of the country can no longer be permitted to remain underdeveloped, and in consequence there are now put out to the world huge schemes of railway and mining enterprise, for the carrying out of which foreign capital is invested.[3]

Beresford concurred. His only anxiety was the security of investment in provinces outwith the effective authority of a crumbling central government. "Such security can only be found in the reform of the country, which can only be effected through pressure from without; and we further say that the vast preponderance of British interests in China demands that Great Britain shall lead and guide the movement", he concluded.[4]

There are two reasons for introducing Admiral Beresford and Mr Dudgeon here. One is purely pedagogic – even the classics of Marxism seldom offer such a succinct and unvarnished description of the methods and purposes of imperialism. Read and re-read it for a study in the dialectical movement of economic and political domination.

The other is that to stand up, one must first be prostrate – and that was China just fifty years before the formation of the People's Republic.

If Beresford and his ilk today appear as curiosities, at least as far as China is concerned, it is not for any change of heart in either the Chamber of Commerce or the Admiralty in London. Left to their own systemic impulses, they would still be pushing and probing at China, meditating on its dismemberment, weighing the policy options for its internal governance. That they cannot – at least not by the same method nor from the same position of overweening strength – is far from fortuitous: they were defeated and expelled by revolution, and to the extent that commercial interests have secured readmission it is on terms laid down by the sovereign Chinese government for the benefit of its own development.

The captains and the capitalists of high Empire for sure have their descendants today, and they have their own non-benevolent ambitions for China. But now it is the CPC that speaks to them from a position of strength. And China's people have been the beneficiaries of the change, along almost every index of human well-being.

The Chinese people's welfare in the here-and-now did not enter into Beresford's calculations, although Victorian imperialism did express care for their souls in the after-life, trade being followed not just by the flag but by a flotilla of Christian missionaries, many of whom caused disruption out of all proportion to their success rate.

But then the Beresfords were not much interested in the well-being of the working people of Britain either. *Plus ca change*. Consider the Covid pandemic. The Chinese state did not act as the compliant servant of capital accumulation. At the outset and throughout, its priority was clearly saving the lives of Chinese people by all possible measures, regardless of the economic consequences. Needless to say, this was quite different from the conduct of the public power in Britain or the US, which was instead marked by corruption, grifting and an insouciant disregard for life.

China put its people's interests first. Now that is standing up.

China in the World

The world policy of the Chinese state has gone through several modifications since 1949. Initially, it aligned closely with the Soviet Union, fought the US to a stand-still in Korea and played a full part in the world Communist movement while paying particular attention to trying to rally the nations just emerging from colonial rule into a common front. In short, it behaved as Johnnie Campbell anticipated in 1949.

China and the USSR fell out in the early 1960s, codifying their differences in a series of ideological polemics that now have an archaic quality, if still replete with points of interest. In 1974 Mao Zedong sent Deng Xiaoping to the United Nations General Assembly, making China's belated debut in that body, to declare the socialist community "no longer in existence", which wasn't correct, but it was by then categorically separated from its erstwhile largest component state, something which surely hastened its actual demise fifteen years later.

That was not all Deng said on that occasion:

> China is not a superpower, nor will she ever seek to be one… If one day China should change her colour and turn into a superpower, if she too should play the tyrant in the world, and everywhere subject others to her bullying, aggression and exploitation, the people of the world should identify her as social-imperialism,[5] expose it, oppose it and work together with the Chinese people to overthrow it.[6]

It is doubtful if any other state in history has ever announced before such an assembly that it should be overthrown by internal and external forces without delay should it start misbehaving. In the fifty years since, the world has never had cause to call in Deng's offer. Rather, Mao's epigrammatic summation of Chinese foreign policy – "Dig tunnels deep, store grain everywhere, and never seek hegemony" – has been followed consistently.

Despite all vicissitudes, and there have been some, and through the years when China sometimes appeared to avoid overtly challenging US strategic interests, followed by the years when China trod very softly in world affairs, these guidelines have set the course for China in the world. Decoded, they mean practising strategic defence, developing economic self-sufficiency and eschewing the politics of domination. In 2024, China is building up vast stockpiles of grain against the possibilities of economic warfare being waged against it by the United States.[7]

That is not to assert more continuity than there is. In 1974 Deng also invoked the Lenin-by-way-of-Mao slogan "Countries want independence, nations want liberation and the people want revolution – this is the irresistible trend of history". History may indeed be irresistible, but it is not a force external to human agency, which pushes it this way and that, in unanticipated forms. For all the fulminations against the USSR, the leadership of the CPC surely did not anticipate its collapse in the form it took, and this was a circumstance which could not be ignored – the enhanced opening to market forces and deeper integration with the capitalist world economy initiated by Deng in 1992 followed directly on the end of Soviet power.

That event forced adjustments on every player on the world stage, ushering in as it did the "unipolar moment" when all issues apparently lay within the grasp of the USA for their determination. That "moment" should be remembered above all as a time of endless wars of intervention. Part of the global significance of the PRC is that it took part in none of them and always sought peaceful dialogue in preference.

Unipolarity is now passing. Already weakened by US military defeats in Iraq and Afghanistan and the disastrous consequences of 'Washington consensus' economics leading to the banking collapse of 2008, it now faces a systemic negation. That is due not only to the decline of the USA, now reflected in its intractable internal turmoil, but also to the peaceful rise of China.

Global multipolarity means many countries of Africa, Asia and South America now have socio-economic options that they did not enjoy previously. They have more room to shape their own futures. All this creates the possibility of a more equal world, with a lessening of the gross economic disparities that have been a central feature of the imperialist era. This emerging multipolarity has China as its spine, an alternative source of investment, credit and diplomatic support, with the infrastructure projects of the Belt and Road Initiative as its visible expression rather than the globe-girdling military bases and massive war fleets which make the US world order manifest.

This Chinese policy is not the way of the past, to be sure. Revolutionary movements can no longer expect the kind of Chinese support they might have been able to expect in the past, although non-interference in the affairs of others is a very long-standing principle, and a good one too. The bourgeoisie has nothing to fear from China other than the success of its example and loss of global hegemony. Nor is the new approach always unproblematic in itself. The Chinese government is not a charity, and there is no doubt that some countries have become over-indebted to Beijing, with whom they still prefer to deal when the IMF and other instruments of US hegemony are the alternative.

Moreover, the stupendous growth of China has not been without consequences for the international working-class. By "opening up" to foreign capital, making available to it much cheaper labour than in the historic centres of the world economy, it helped ignite a process leading to the devastation of industrial communities and the decline of effective trade unionism in much of Europe and North America, while allowing international monopolies to drive the profit share of GDP to record highs. For sure, the Communist Party of China is first of all answerable to the Chinese people alone for the impact of its policy; it is not responsible for the failure of the working class in the west to make socialist revolution (or even maintain Keynesian economic strategies); and the lifting of hundreds of millions of Chinese workers and peasants out of poverty weighs more heavily in the scale of human progress; but this is a negative consequence of China's rise which cannot be overlooked in an assessment of the global impact of the PRC if truth is to be sought from facts. Paradoxically, had socialism in fact prevailed in Britain and similar developed countries, the vast infusions of foreign capital into China would have been unlikely to have occurred. The advance of a prosperous China, a historic gain in and of itself, has been at the price of prosperity elsewhere because it has been conducted in significant part through integration into the bourgeois world economy of monopoly capital, a peculiar expression of the law of uneven development.

Notwithstanding, the alternative world order promoted by the Chinese government offers cooperation and development for all and eschews militarism and interference. It prioritises adherence to international law and peaceful resolution of disputes. This is not the world order of imperialism, and its methods are not those of Beresford and Dudgeon, nor Bush and Blair come to that – pressure, threats, looting and diktat.

That should not be a remarkable development, but it is.

Chinese Socialism

Most serious socialists in Britian would know something about the story of the Paris Commune of 1871, and some would know quite a lot.

Yet many would likely greet any mention of the Taiping rebellion with a blank stare, although it was an event which happened just a few years earlier and was of an incomparably greater scale and duration, and cost many millions of lives as against the 30,000 martyrs of the Commune.

For all its pseudo-Christian precepts and fairly crude utopianism, the rebellion was a mass peasant movement with a marked (primitive) communistic orientation. The Taiping regime, with a leadership "mostly from the so-called lower classes", established a trade monopoly, fed at least 400,000 mouths every month from public stores, proposed eliminating taxes in favour of the transfer of surpluses (over and above what a peasant family immediately needed) to a public treasury, and endeavoured to divide land on an egalitarian basis, including between men and women. It promised far more than it delivered and was in the end crushed by the imperial authorities just as surely as the Parisian workers, but its aspiration was certainly communistic.[8]

There is an almost ecumenical consensus on that point. The Catholic

Monsignor Rizzolati wrote to his superiors in France that "all my priests, both European and Chinese, describe the rebels as the propagators of the most frightful communism", plundering "the most opulent families and persons."

From the Anglican side, the Reverend W.H. Medhurst reported a discussion with a rebel who averred that "all monies, immediately they were acquired, were instantly to be handed over to the general treasury, and any person secretly hoarding wealth is suspected of treasonable practices". Nearly ten years later, in 1861, another cleric, the Rev. Griffith John wrote that "the system of community of goods still continues... everything is in common, they have no salary".

This appreciation had secular endorsement too. The imperialist solider Garnett Wolseley (Crimean War, Indian rebellion of 1857, Sudan War) found himself in China in 1860, fighting the Second Opium War in the interests of free trade and drug addiction. He observed that in Nanjing "it would appear almost as if they wished to abolish altogether the use of coin, and reduce society to that patriarchal state in which the people receive their daily food, clothing & co, and have all their ordinary wants of nature supplied by the master under whose banner they served".[9]

Much more could be said, but the relevant point should be clear – Chinese socialism, and indeed Mao Zedong Thought, have their own indigenous antecedents, different from but not necessarily inferior to, those of European socialism, less rooted in proletarian experience and informed by frankly deluded ideological propositions on occasion, but greater by far in scope, violent expression and immediate ambition. And the bourgeois of the time recognised this, even if much of the workers' movement remained in ignorance.

So we should not try to squeeze the experience of Chinese socialism into straitjackets of European experience. When Lenin told his victorious Bolsheviks in 1918 that the Russian Communists stood on the shoulders of the Paris Commune and the experience of the pre-war German Social Democratic Party he was saying something entirely unintelligible to the vast majority of contemporary Chinese, and invoking episodes which have scarcely had much relevance to them since (although it is worth noting that several early Chinese communists, including Zhou Enlai and Deng Xiaoping, spent time in France in the early 1920s and would in the course of their political work have come into contact with, and absorbed key ideas from, the European Marxist tradition).

The Communist Party of China was founded, as it declares, as a consequence of the October Revolution and under the guidance of the Communist International. That was the start, and not the end of the story. Mechanically reproducing experience elsewhere proved not to work. Basing strategy on the realities of the Chinese people's rich history of elemental struggle, from the Taiping Rebellion to the Yi Ho Tuan (Boxer) Uprising, the

1911 revolution overthrowing the Manchus and the May 4th movement did (eventually), uniting peasant discontent with national aspirations within a global proletarian movement.

The CPC has since championed the 'sinification of Marxism', an idea which bears two meanings. The first is that it consists of the application of Marxism as a given set of principles to the particular social conditions of China. Mao Zedong and his comrades set about this work – they placed the peasantry at the centre of communist politics as a revolutionary subject, and developed the concept of 'new democracy' among other innovations. These are of enduring importance.

The second meaning posits the transformation of Marxism itself through the experience and reflection of the Chinese people (more than one-fifth of humanity), Chinese traditions and the Chinese Revolution. In this understanding, China takes Marxism from the European labour movement and returns it to the world enriched, developed and nearer to universalisation, but not, of course, 'finished', something which would be entirely impossible.

A recent official publication of the CPC puts it thus: 'The history of the Communist Party of China was formerly the history of the localisation of Marxism in China, but from now on it will be the history of the development of Chinese Marxism.'[10] Here is the inversion of subject and object, from the local application of the Marxism of Lenin and the Communist International to developing a new and distinctive Marxism that will doubtless have lessons for the rest of the world, albeit not as a new model.

It introduces novel philosophical elements into Marxism, supplementing Hegel's method with ideas from the Confucian and other Chinese canons. Some of this sounds quite alien to western class-struggle socialism, but demystified it is not necessarily at odds. For example, the CPC champions "common prosperity" and a "harmonious society". An ordinary person in Britain may easily identify those as features of a socialist society, and certainly they are not attributes of contemporary Britain or the USA at all.

That is not to say that all such theoretical innovations are necessarily fruitful, and the integration of Confucianism into Communism definitely has its limits – the "eight honours and eight disgraces" promoted in the time of Hu Jintao as party leader read as little more than a Scout's Oath, and are a sorry contrast to the richness of the ideological cadre formation set out in Liu Shaoqi's *How to be a Good Communist*.[11] However, to deny the possibility of Marxism drawing in its development from philosophical resources outside Europe and beyond the reach of Marx and Engels in their time risks collapsing into both dogmatism and Eurocentrism.

Since the present system in China does not correspond to past models of socialism, some deny its socialist character *tout court*. It is, of course, somewhat arrogant to dismiss the views of the Chinese state and ruling party altogether. However, there are points which cannot be overlooked –

the dizzying levels of income inequality, the persistence of unemployment and the intrusion of market relationships into basic public services (all unknown in Mao's time) – and which must raise questions. Yet the present CPC leadership – and here it is at one with Mao – insists that moving a huge and originally very poor country into a fully socialist society is the work of many generations.[12] And the complete elimination of absolute poverty, a recent achievement of the CPC, is not just a staggering achievement, it is a socialist one.

The international context is critical too. The victory of the Russian Revolution and international communist leadership enabled the CPC and the Chinese revolution to retain an overall working-class character and socialist orientation even as it fought for national independence and new democracy in isolation, for the most part, from the anyway small Chinese working class.

The global movement gave a decisive imprint to events, at the same time as the Mao leadership adapted its general principles to Chinese circumstances. It may be that the Chinese revolution, and the form it took, is the greatest and most enduring consequence of the October Revolution.

Today, Chinese society must perforce develop in a world in which socialism has otherwise very largely disappeared as a systemic alternative and the world communist movement is a shadow of its former force, when rapidly extending prosperity was indispensable for legitimising rule by a Communist party and when no world economic alternative existed to capitalism any longer.

That is not to argue that the idea of socialism can be liquidated into purely pragmatic adaptations or stuck as a label on any old project when deemed convenient. It must have universal, if evolving, characteristics, and ultimately aim at the supersession of the law of value and the regulating role of commodity relationships, while empowering working people and eliminating first exploiting classes and then all class distinctions. Most of that work remains ahead in China. But hitherto, no more than the foundational steps have been successfully taken in those directions in any socialist society, and attempts to force the issue, buttressed by bombastic claims of the attainment of stages in fact barely glimpsed, have led only to subsequent retreats and even collapse.

That the PRC has avoided that over 75 years – or rather, has corrected course when it had to – is a deeply significant episode in world socialist history. It has now outlasted the Soviet Union's seventy-four year existence.

So Chinese socialism cannot be judged exclusively by the application of concepts developed in other civilisations and other centuries, even as it does not insist on the universal validity of its own model. It can and should be critically analysed, but the main thing is that it exists, develops and grows, not as the "beleaguered fortress" of Soviet Russia did, but as an extremely influential and dynamic contribution to human civilisation.

The future of socialism in the world depends very heavily on developments in China and on the leadership of its communist party. As Xi Jinping has said, without China, socialism risked being pushed entirely to the margins of world affairs after 1991. Xi also stresses the socialist essence of China's state, the continuity of today's China with the revolution of 75 years ago and opposition to a nihilistic view of Soviet experience. He likewise emphasises the 'final goal' of communism.

All that more than suffices to make the world ideologically multipolar, as well as in terms of the distribution of power which China has altered irreversibly. It is not the zero-sum ideological confrontation of the Soviet period, but China's path challenges the hegemony of the capitalist system and of neoliberal centrism. The *Communique on the Current State of the Ideological Sphere*, issued by the CPC in 2014, makes clear, *inter alia*, the party's opposition to "the promotion of neoliberalism", equated with "market omnipotence" and "total privatisation", and also blamed for "calamitous consequences" for countries all over the world and for the "international financial crisis".[13]

After 75 years, the Peoples Republic of China therefore stands at the very heart of an alternative to the world of the Washington Consensus, the militarised "New World Order" and economic crisis and chaos. The alternative itself is unfinished and perhaps unfinishable, but China is holding the door open to *possibilities* beyond the status quo, to a menu of other options for humanity.

That is most likely the most profound global significance of the PRC on its 75th birthday.

NOTES

1. The author first heard this story in 1978 from Monty Goldman, a leading Communist in east London, who used it to contrast disappointing local election results with the contemporaneous triumph of the Saur [or April] revolution in Afghanistan.
2. *I* by Lord Charles Beresford (Harper Brothers, London/New York: 1900)
3. Beresford, p 85
4. Ibid. P 96
5. The pejorative term then used by the CPC to describe the Soviet Union – "socialism in words, imperialism in deeds."
6. Speech By Chairman of the Delegation of the People's Republic of China, Deng Xiaoping, at the Special Session of the U.N. General Assembly (marxists.org)
7. See 'Why is Xi Jinping building secret commodity stockpiles?', *The Economist* 23 July 2024
8. See *The Taiping Revolutionary Movement* by Chien Yuwen (Yale, New Haven/London: 1973) pp 143-45 and *Taiping Rebellion* 1850-1864 by J.C. Chang (Hong Kong: 1963) pp ix, 39
9. From *Western Reports on the Taiping* by Prescott Clarke and J.S. Gregory (Croom Helm, London, 1982), pp 84, 87-88, 267 and 331.
10. *An Ideological History of the Communist Party of China*: Volume 3 by Wu Guoyou and Ding Xuemei, trans. Sun Li and Shelly Bryant (Royal Collins, 2020), p. 7.
11. Liu was number two to Mao in the CPC and the PRC from 1949 to 1966, when he fell victim to the Cultural Revolution. He was posthumously rehabilitated in 1980.
12. In 1963 the CPC stated "socialist society covers a very long historical period…a very long period of time is needed to decide 'who will win' in the struggle between socialism and capitalism. Several decades won't do it; success requires anywhere from one to several centuries […] it is better to prepare for a longer rather than a shorter period of time." Communist Party of China, 'On Khrushchev's Phoney Communism', in *The Polemic on the General Line of the International Communist Movement* (1964; Red Star Press, 1976), p. 471-72
13. *The Political Thought of Xi Jinping* by Steve Tsang and Olivia Cheung (OUP Oxford: 2024) pp 82-83

4

The significance of China's fulfilment of its Second Centenary Goal by 2049

Cheng Enfu and Chen Jian[1]

Under the leadership of the Communist Party of China (CPC), the Chinese nation has overcome the bitter modern history of a semi-feudal and semi-colonial society, and finally established a New China in 1949, which not only washed away the humiliation of being constantly invaded by the imperialist powers, but also initiated a brand-new situation of striving to become stronger and more powerful.

Nowadays, on the basis of fully realising the first goal of building a moderately prosperous society in all respects by the centenary of the CPC (founded in 1921), the second goal of building China into a modern socialist country that is prosperous, strong, democratic, culturally advanced, harmonious and beautiful by the centenary of the People's Republic of China is being rapidly realised. In this paper, we will analyse the significance of China's realisation of the second centenary goal in economic, political and international dimensions.

1. Continuously surpassing the United States in various economic respects and become the world's largest economy and a 'Top Country in the Centre'

President Xi Jinping pointed out that "China enjoys distinct strengths such as a socialist market economy in systemic terms, a supersize market in terms of demand, a full-fledged industrial system in terms of supply, and abundant, high-calibre labour forces and entrepreneurs in terms of human resources."[2] These advantages constitute a solid support for China's transformation from a follower to a leader in the world economy.

First, the growth rate of China's economy since 1949 suggests that it will surpass the United States by 2049.

The history of China since 1949 can be divided into three major stages: before reform and opening-up, after reform and opening-up but before the 18th CPC National Congress, and in the New Era after the 18th CPC National Congress. In these three stages "three miracles" in world economic development have been created, and they correspond consecutively to the formation of a preliminarily rich and strong economy, a secondarily rich and strong country, and an intermediately rich and strong country as a quasi-centre in the world's economic system.

The first miracle of creating a preliminarily rich and strong China was achieved before reform and opening-up. The founding of New China put a definitive end to the semi-colonial and semi-feudal state of poverty and weakness in China, and to the frequent wars that the country had suffered for more than 100 years since the First Opium War. Under the leadership of the CPC, the great socialist practice and exploration of China began in a poor and backward country. Science and technology began to develop as marked by the "two bombs (nuclear bomb and missile) and one satellite project"; an independent industrial and national economic system was initially established; comprehensive development was seen in education, culture, health and sports; the population grew rapidly and people's livelihood significantly improved; China successfully restored its legitimate seat in the United Nations (UN) and its Security Council; and China had a great influence among the vast number of third-world countries. All these show that New China got rid of the image of a poor and weak country of the old China in international economic, political and military arenas, and truly stood up and became preliminarily rich and strong. This is the "first miracle" in the economic development of New China.

Statistics for this stage show that while in 1952, China's GDP was only RMB 67.9 billion yuan, it was as high as 364.52 billion yuan in 1978. In terms of the year-by-year development rate, although there was a decline in China's economic growth in 1960, 1961, 1962, 1967, 1968, and 1976, respectively, due to natural disasters, policy mistakes and exceptional circumstances, China's average nominal annual growth rate during the period of 1952-1978 was still as high as 6.68 percent. In 1952, China's total population (excluding Hong Kong, Macao, and Taiwan) amounted to 575 million, and per capita GDP was 119.4 yuan. In 1978, per capita GDP rose to 381 yuan, even with the total population jumping to 960 million, and the average annual growth rate of per capita GDP was as high as 4.56 percent between 1952-1978. During this period, the average annual growth rate of China's real GDP was as high as 6.15 percent, and the average annual growth rate of real per capita GDP was as high as 4.05 percent. With the average growth rate of the world economy during this period being 3 percent, China's development rate was more than twice that of the world.[3]

The second miracle was created after reform and opening-up as a stage of becoming intermediately rich and strong. The convening of the Third Plenary Session of the Eleventh CPC Central Committee in 1978 marked the entry of China's socialist practice into a new period of reform and opening-up. By 2012, China's industrial output value and foreign exchange reserves had jumped to first place in the world; its total economic output steadily ranked second in the world; the development of education, culture, health and sports were remarkable; people's livelihoods were raised from subsistence to moderate prosperity; Hong Kong and Macao were successfully returned to China; and China's political and military status were rising internationally. These changes indicated that China is in the position of a "secondarily rich and strong" country. It is the "second miracle" of China's economic development.

The third economic miracle has been created in the New Era, with the formation of a "quasi-centre" in the world economic system at the stage of becoming intermediately rich and strong. Since the 18th CPC National Congress, the CPC Central Committee, with Comrade Xi Jinping at its core, has adjusted the direction in the advance of the CPC and the state and ushered in a new era of socialism with Chinese characteristics. With the changes in the main contradiction in China's society, the central task of the Party and the country has been further enriched and upgraded while continuing to focus on "economic construction as the centre". Through implementing the "people-centred" development philosophy, the "Five-Sphere Integrated Plan", and the "Four-Pronged Comprehensive Strategy", and through integrating "the great struggle, the great project, the great cause and the great dream", the comprehensive development of human beings and the sharing of wealth among all people have been continuously advanced. Furthermore, through international cooperation such as the Belt and Road Initiative (BRI), BRICS (Brazil, Russia, India, China and South Africa), the SCO (Shanghai Cooperation Organisation), AIIB (Asian Infrastructure Investment Bank) etc., China has contributed Chinese wisdom and provided Chinese solutions for human development, and promoted the construction of a community of shared future for humanity. With its growing international appeal and influence, China has become a "quasi-centre" country in the world system,[4] marking China's status as an "intermediately rich and strong" country, and is presenting the "third miracle" in new China's economic development.

Relevant statistics and forecast data also support the above assertion on China's development stage. Since its reform and opening-up, China's economy has been developing rapidly, with the average annual growth rate of the country's GDP as high as 9.4 percent from 1978 to 2023, as a result of which, China's total GDP in 2023 was $17.52 trillion, with a growth rate of 5.2 percent, while the total GDP of the United States in 2023 was $27.36 trillion with a growth rate of 2.54 percent.[5] These figures visually and powerfully demonstrate that China's economic growth rate since the founding of New China has exceeded that of almost all capitalist countries, which vividly illustrates the historic achievements of China's economic development.

Second, China is able to achieve step by step its centenary goal of moving from its current position of a "quasi-centre" in the world's economic system to that of a "top centre".

Relevant data calculations show that if China basically realises modernisation in 2035, it will be a "second-highest rich and strong" country in the "centre" of the world economic system; if it realises full modernisation in 2049, it will be a rich and strong country ranking among the "top countries" in the centre of the world economic system. Assuming that by 2049 China's total population reaches 1.3 billion people, that of the United States reaches 335 million people, the exchange rate remains unchanged, with China's total GDP of $17.52 trillion and US total GDP of $27.36 trillion in 2023, and assuming after calculation 5 percent for China's annual GDP growth and 2.5 percent for the United States in 2024–2049, then through comprehensive calculation we can derive that by 2049 China's total GDP and per capita GDP volume would be $59.94 trillion and $46,106.52, respectively, compared to that of the United States in the amount of $49.69 trillion and $148,300.[6]

At present, China is focusing on building a new development pattern with the domestic macro-cycle as the main body facilitated by the mutually reinforcing domestic and international dual cycles. China is accelerating the development of new quality productive forces represented by artificial intelligence (AI), and emphasising the opening-up strategy with the advantage of independent intellectual property rights rather than the outdated opening-up strategy of leveraging comparative advantages. Through implementing a new type of national system of self-reliance in key and core technologies, the government is clarifying the direction for promoting high-quality development of China's economy and society. Even if the US-led West launches a cool war, a cold war or a hot war against China, and keeps increasing illegal sanctions to the extent of a total blockade, China will be able to unite the vast number of developing countries and the countries of the South to fully realise the second centenary goal in a self-reliant manner. China can confidently turn the negative things of the US-led West that aim to suppress China and of various "hybrid wars" against China into positive things of accelerated modernisation and earlier unification of China. Strengthening the county and the army requires a strengthening of heart and spirit first. In that line, China can confidently turn the bad things that the US and the West do to suppress China and launch all kinds of "hybrid wars" into the good things of accelerated modernisation and early unification of China, thus achieving a strong county, prosperous people and modern Chinese civilisation.

2. Continuously surpassing the West in various political respects and fully demonstrating the advantages of whole process People's Democracy

Democracy is a common value shared by all humankind and is the fruit of the development of human political civilisation. There is no end to the human exploration and practice of democracy. By 2049, the systemic advantages and practical effects of China's socialist whole process people's democracy will certainly be better demonstrated.

First, the people have not only the right to vote in various ways, but also the right to broad participation.

When the people have the right to vote, they can freely express their personal will, but the right to vote alone is not enough, because the right to political equality of "one person, one vote" does not automatically eliminate other political inequalities and inequalities in economic and social rights. In order to solve this problem, the people must have the right to participate in a comprehensive and wide-ranging manner. The right to participation lies at the core of democracy. A democracy is only formalistic if the people only have the right to vote but not the right to extensive participation, and if the people are awakened only when they vote and go dormant afterward. The most important thing is that the people are able to participate deeply in the management of the life of the state and society through both elections and means other than elections.

Furthermore, in accordance with the law, the Chinese people have the right to participate in the management of state and social affairs and of economic and cultural undertakings through various means and forms, such as consultations, expert seminars, consultation meetings, debates, symposia, hearings, councils, criticisms and suggestions. It can be seen that the people of China have not only the right to vote, but also the right to participate in a wide range of activities; not only to express their democratic will effectively, but also to fully exercise their right to democratic participation in democratic elections, democratic consultation, democratic decision-making, democratic management and democratic supervision.

Second, when the people are promised something verbally during the election process, those promises are largely fulfilled after the election.

Is it necessary to make verbal promises to the people during the election process? The answer is yes, because this is not only a conventional practice, but also the presentation of a future plan and a people-friendly attitude. However, verbal promises in the election process are not the objective of democracy; the objective of democracy should be the transformation of verbal promises into real actions. If the people are awakened only at the time of voting and then go dormant, if they only listen to flowery slogans during the election campaign and then have no say in it, if they are favoured only during canvassing and then left out in the cold after the election, then this kind of democracy is not a real democracy. It is clear that the CPC and the government must take effective action to continuously respond to the needs and aspirations of the people after making verbal promises.

The CPC and the government of China have a strong sense of continuous attention and response to the people's interests and needs. This is because the democratic chain in China is complete, covering the entire process of the five major democratic processes of democratic election, democratic consultation, democratic decision-making, democratic management and democratic supervision. Thus a systematic "full-chain democracy" has been formed, which overcomes the "half democracy" that emphasises election but not management. The undesirable phenomenon and embarrassing situation of democracy at the time of election but no democracy after the election has been avoided. This ensures that the verbal promises made to the Chinese people during the election process will be realised after the election.

Third, it is important to pay close attention to what kind of political procedures and rules are stipulated in the systems and laws, but also, and even more importantly, to see whether or not these systems and laws are actually implemented.

The vitality of systems and laws lies not only in the possession of basic political procedures and rules, but also in their eventual implementation and effectiveness. Only in this way can they take root, blossom and bear fruit. If the system and the law are just for show and cannot be effectively implemented, then they will exist in name only.

The political procedures and rules laid down in China's system and laws are very strict. For example, if we look at the procedures through which members of the National People's Congress are elected, we will find that it takes various forms, including initial inspection and consultation, preparatory elections, secret ballot elections, and competitive elections. These cover both top-down organisational nominations and bottom-up free elections and constitute real and concrete procedural democracy. Moreover, under the principle of democratic centralism, China's system and laws have the advantage of being implemented on a national basis. Therefore, in the future, China will gradually and truly achieve unity between the expression of public opinions and the satisfaction of public opinion, thus realising democracy with strong executive power and highly effective overall performance.

Fourth, we should focus not only on whether the rules and procedures for the operation of power are democratic, but also on whether power is truly subject to supervision and constraint by the people.

The people are the legitimate source of all state power. Since power originates from the people and is endowed by the people, it can only be used to serve, benefit and be accountable to the people. Therefore, the people should constitute the main body of supervision and constraint of power. Numerous historical experiences have shown that the less power is effectively supervised and restrained, the greater the possibility of abuse and corruption. Only when power is truly subject to the people's all-round strict supervision and regulation can it effectively fulfil its important role.

After years of practice and improvement, China has basically established the institutional, procedural and standardised rules for the operation of power, which further enhances the vitality and anti-corruption character of power, while in the meantime avoiding both "uncaged" power and power locked up in the cage of capital. For example, China is: 1) establishing and implementing a system whereby those in power dare not be corrupt, those who are corrupt will be severely punished, and active and passive bribery will be combated; 2) improving the system for transparency in party, government and judicial affairs, as well as in administrative procedures of all areas; 3) perfecting the system for questioning, accountability, auditing of economic responsibility, and blame-taking resignation and removal from office. At the same time, systems of internal Party supervision, internal political supervision, supervision by the National People's Congress, supervision by democratic parties, supervision by the people without party affiliation, supervision by scientists, and supervision by the masses have been proposed and implemented, allowing power to operate in a transparent way. In the long run, this multifaceted system of supervision and regulation in China will effectively carry forward the fine traditional style of the ruling party, whereby the National People's Congress and the people's government keep close contact with the masses using the method of self-criticism and self-revolution.

The Constitution of the Communist Party of China, adopted at the Twentieth Party Congress in October 2022, states that the Party "shall uphold and improve the people's congress system, the Communist Party-led system of multiparty cooperation and political consultation, the system of regional ethnic autonomy, and the system of public self-governance at the primary level. The Party shall develop a broader, fuller, and more robust whole-process people's democracy, advance extensive, multilevel, and institutionalised development of consultative democracy, and act in earnest to protect the people's right to manage state and social affairs and to manage economic and cultural matters."[7] We firmly believe that it is necessary to dispel the "superstition of Western-style democracy" and the "cult of Western-style system" represented by the United States, and unswervingly hold high the scientific banner of whole-process people's democracy in the future. Also, we must better transform the advantages of the system into efficacy in governance. We will then be able to, by the middle of the 21st century, better win the people's support in continuing to write a new chapter of socialist political civilisation with Chinese characteristics and make new and greater contributions to the development and progress of the political civilisation of mankind.

3. Continuously transcending hegemonism and narrow nationalism at the international level and promoting the building of a community with a shared future for humanity and a new internationalism

Looking around the globe, the world today is in the midst of changes of a magnitude unseen in a century. The configuration of international forces has undergone profound changes, and in recent decades a large number of emerging market economies and developing countries have embarked on the fast track of development, leading to the rise of a group of countries whose strength, capacity for independent development and international influence have been continuously enhanced, and who are changing the global political and economic pattern. The "old ways" of Western imperialist countries of relying on hegemony and power politics have become increasingly impractical, as the international system and order are in urgent need of in-depth adjustment in the light of the changes in the international balance of power. The call for promoting the development of the global governance system in the direction of greater justice and rationality has also become increasingly louder. China has always adhered to a foreign policy of peace and justice, standing on the right side of history and on the side of human progress, working with the world's anti-hegemonic forces and people of all countries to push the wheels of history towards a brighter future, and contributing China's solutions for the realisation of the overall interests of humankind.

First, China has always had the tradition of uniting countries of the Global South.

A country should not be guided by the pursuit of profit, but by the pursuit of the greater good and shared interest, which is particularly true in international cooperation. As the world's largest developing country, China has always adhered to the concept of truthfulness and sincerity and attaches great importance to friendly and cooperative relations with the vast number of developing countries. As an active participant in international cooperation, China has always had a tradition of solidarity with the countries of the South, and the vast number of developing countries are natural allies in the development of China's cause of diplomacy. In the process of South-South cooperation, China has insisted on mutual support and assistance with the vast number of countries in the South, and China's infrastructure construction has been incorporated into projects such as transportation and railroads building in many brotherly countries. On the journey to fully realise its second centenary goal, China has the strength and ability to unite and help more developing countries embark on the path to modernisation and national prosperity, and to promote South-South cooperation.

Second, China is a country that stands on the side of justice.

Today, the changes in the world and in history are unfolding in an unprecedented manner. The question of peace or war, cooperation or confrontation, is an important one facing every country and the world. The founding of New China was like the morning sun piercing through the fog and illuminating the future of peace and development. Now, after more than 70 years of development, China has become a powerful force for world peace. China's development has not only brought peace and prosperity to its own people, but also injected new impetus into the cause of global peace and development. Unlike countries that stand on the opposite side on the question of world peace, China has always been its guardian. The Chinese nation has been a peace-loving people since ancient times, and Chinese civilisation has an outstanding peaceful nature, passing on the concepts of "peace is precious", "being a good and friendly neighbour", and "building a commonwealth of the world" from generation to generation. Therefore, China has always stood on the side of justice and fairness, maintaining peace and promoting development while taking into account the legitimate concerns of other countries, contributing Chinese wisdom and Chinese solutions to the harmonious development of international relations and the peaceful development of the international environment.

Certain Western countries not only eye China's development with hostility, but also try to manipulate attitudes and opinions of other countries by making absurd and ill-grounded statements. China, however, has proved to the world through its practical actions that it has always pursued a defensive national policy. China's development represents the growth of peace in the world. The more China develops, the more the world develops. No matter how far it develops, China will never claim hegemony. On the one hand, with regards to its attitude towards international affairs, China always decides its position and policy on the basis of the facts of the matter itself, upholds the basic norms of international relations, and safeguards international justice; on the other hand, in its attitude towards other countries, China has always insisted on the equality of all countries, irrespective of their size, strength, and wealth, and has respected the sovereignty and territorial integrity of each country and its path to development and the social system that has been chosen by its people independently. China resolutely opposes all forms of hegemonism, imperialism, neo-colonialism, neo-fascism, and neo-liberalism. It is also against the Cold War mindset, interference in other countries' internal affairs, and hypocritical double standards. It is evident to the world that China has always been a builder of world peace, a contributor to global development and a defender of the international order, as codified in the United Nations Charter. China's adherence to the path of peaceful development and its concentration on its own affairs is in itself a major contribution to world peace and development. China insists on developing itself through the maintenance of world peace, never seeking development at the expense of the interests of other countries. China is safeguarding world peace through its own development. It is willing to live in harmony with all peoples of the world, to develop in harmony, to seek, share and protect peace together, and to share with the world the opportunities of China's development.

Third, China advocates the building of a community with a shared future for humanity during the struggles against hegemonism.

China has continuously transcended hegemonism and narrow nationalism to promote the building of a community of shared future for humanity, which is a Chinese-style innovation for realising the prosperity and development of mankind at present, and an exploration of the development of world history on the basis of Marxism and Sinicised Marxism. At the same time, the idea of "a community of shared future for humanity" lies at the core of China's major global initiatives, namely, the BRI, Global Development Initiative, Global Security Initiative, Global Civilisation Initiative, and Global AI Governance Initiative. Among them, the most vivid embodiment of the effective practice of a community with a shared future for humanity is the BRI. The construction of a community with a shared future for humanity was from its very beginning intended to benefit all peoples of the world, promote peace, and thus realise common prosperity and development. For that reason, it was widely welcomed by the international community once it was put forward. As a practical platform for promoting the building of a community with a shared future for humanity, the BRI, while achieving high-quality development, has also demonstrated that this road of hope and happiness embodies the goal of benefiting the whole world, will extend wider and farther in the future, and will ultimately arrive at the final destination of jointly building a prosperous and beautiful world.

The new Marxist internationalism that we advocate has three meanings: first, to promote the development of a community with a shared future for humanity on the basis of the common values of humankind; second, to promote the development of world socialism on the basis of Marxism and the core socialist values; and third, to unite all progressive forces of the world to counter the hegemonic and monopolistic oligarchic forces that are attempting to besiege and annihilate peace-loving countries such as China and the forces of socialism.

NOTES

1. This article is translated from Chinese by Liu Zixu, associate researcher at the Chinese Academy of Social Sciences.
2. "Meeting Challenges with Unity of Purpose To Write a New Chapter for Asia-Pacific Cooperation" (written speech at the APEC CEO Summit), San Francisco, November 16, 2023. Qiushi: http://en.qstheory.cn/2023-11/17/c_939840.htm
3. Cheng Enfu, "The Constitution of China is the Fundamental Legal Basis and Theoretical Crystallization of the Reform and Opening-up: An Interview with Professor Cheng Enfu, Member of the Committee of Education, Science, Culture and Health of the National People's Congress," *Marxism Studies*, no. 11, 2018.
4. Cheng Enfu, "The Great Achievement of Marxism and Its Sinicized Theories: Xi Jinping's Economic Thought on Socialism with Chinese Characteristics for a New Era," *Southeast Academia*, no. 5, 2018, pp. 1–8.
5. "GDP Expands 5.25 in 2023 – Analyzing China's Key Economic Indicators." *China Briefing*, https://www.china-briefing.com/news/chinas-gdp-in-2023/
6. Ibid.
7. *Qiushi*. http://en.qstheory.cn/2023-01/06/c_845465.htm.

THIS PAGE INTENTIONALLY LEFT BLANK

5

The 'primary stage of socialism' in historical context

Kenny Coyle

China's advance over the past 75 years is historically unprecedented. Yet, paradoxically, for some sections of the left this transformation has been the result of the triumph of capitalism not the success of socialism. Many socialists who might otherwise deny the possibility of a capitalist system achieving social and economic progress anywhere else, find no contradiction in crediting capitalism with raising China's GDP from $218 billion in 1978 to $17.52 trillion in 2023 and raising 800 million people out of absolute poverty thereby overcoming generations of backwardness inherited from its pre-1949 semi-colonial and semi-feudal status.

Certainly, glaring contradictions exist. Social inequality in China is stark, perhaps not surprising given the country's highly uneven and unbalanced growth since 1978, but the Chinese leadership has placed increasing emphasis on the need to rebalance development to secure 'common prosperity'.

Comparisons with pre-1978 China and with the experiences of socialism elsewhere inevitably lead to questions over whether today's China possesses sufficiently socialist credentials. However, this comparison cuts both ways. Soviet and other European socialist systems did not survive and China itself was at risk of being toppled in 1989. However, if longer and better lives is a fundamental index of social progress, China stands tall. Average life expectancy is 78 years old (13 years longer than in 1980) for a Chinese citizen, outstripping the USA (76) and Russia (69).

China has learned, primarily from its own experiences, but also from international practice, to chart its own path toward socialism. This does not devalue the experience of others, or of previous Chinese generations, but rather it is the adaptation and development of all that is rich and valuable in each of them.

Chinese communists have developed their theory and practice through the creative application of Marxist principles to national conditions, and the concept of the 'primary stage of socialism' provides a foundation stone for understanding "socialism with Chinese characteristics".

The primary stage – a definition

The Communist Party of China (CPC) constitution offers a useful summary of the understanding that the primary stage is a reflection of objective economic and cultural reality. Its key points are that it will take at least a century for China to complete the major tasks of this primary stage, which derive from fundamental Chinese material realities.

> China is currently in the primary stage of socialism and will remain so for a long time to come. This is a stage of history that cannot be bypassed as China, which used to be economically and culturally lagging, makes progress in socialist modernisation; it will take over a century. China's development of socialism must begin from China's own circumstances, follow the path of socialism with Chinese characteristics, and comprehensively promote national rejuvenation through the path of Chinese modernisation. At the present stage, the principal contradiction in Chinese society is that between the ever-growing needs of the people for a better life and unbalanced and inadequate development. Owing to both domestic factors and international influences, a certain amount of class struggle will continue to exist for a long time to come, and under certain circumstances may even grow more pronounced, however, it is no longer the principal contradiction. In building socialism in China, the basic tasks are to further release and develop the productive forces and gradually achieve socialist modernisation and, to this end, reform those elements and areas within the relations of production and the superstructure that are unsuited to the development of the productive forces. The Party must uphold and improve the basic economic systems including the system under which public ownership is the mainstay and diverse forms of ownership develop together, a system under which

distribution according to work is the mainstay while multiple forms of distribution exist alongside it, and the socialist market economy.[1]

How does this approach correspond to previous debates about the nature of socialism and socialist construction within the Marxist tradition?

1] Initial foundations – Marx and Engels

Using the insights of historical materialism, Marx and Engels were able not only to analyse existing capitalist societies but also pre-capitalist formations.[2] However, they could only forecast the most general contours of communist society that lay somewhere in the future. From the *Communist Manifesto* onward, Marx and Engels avoided detailed blueprints for this society that was yet to come. The *Manifesto* itself outlined a limited 10-point programme, including such points as nationalisation of the land, creation of a national state bank, etc., which would allow a successful communist-led revolution see the working class consolidate itself through a series of steps as the leading class, over an undetermined period.

The experience of the Paris Commune of 1871, the only example of the 'dictatorship of the proletariat' available for study during their lifetimes, was extremely limited in terms of its longevity, geographical remit and governance capacity. It was also hampered by the indecision of an ideologically diffuse leadership. Nonetheless the political lessons were immense and, while Engels later noted that "in the economic sphere much was left undone which, according to our view today, the Commune ought to have done",[3] the Commune did begin to implement substantial social reforms.[4]

With very limited practical experience to draw on, Marx famously distinguished between the lower (usually referred to as socialist) and higher stages of communism, the first stage being:

> a communist society, not as it has developed on its own foundations, but, on the contrary, just as it emerges from capitalist society; which is thus in every respect, economically, morally, and intellectually, still stamped with the birthmarks of the old society from whose womb it emerges… defects are inevitable in the first phase of communist society as it is when it has just emerged after prolonged birth pangs from capitalist society. Right can never be higher than the economic structure of society and its cultural development conditioned thereby.[5]

Marx presents this hypothetical society as having already matured and makes no attempt to guess the precise process or specific stages that precede it, far less offer a timescale for how much time the "prolonged birth pangs" would last. He then offers the following markers that will signify humanity's entrance to full communism, including an end to the "division of labour, and therewith also the antithesis between mental and physical labour" based on increased productive forces to a level of abundance that allows the overcoming of '"bourgeois right'" - the source of inequality in the lower stage of communism that rewards individuals according to work - and allow human beings to live in a society whose maxim is "from each according to their ability, to each according to their needs".[6]

Due to the limitations of concrete historical experience, Marx and Engels left open many questions about the precise steps on this journey from capitalism to communism.

2] Learning from Lenin

Lenin's lifelong contribution to Marxism was immense, but the most important contribution of his later years was his enrichment of Marxist theory by drawing on the tangible experience of the Russian Revolution. Lenin's reflections on the unfolding socialist revolution lifted Marxist analysis of the transition to socialism from abstract assumptions to concrete reality. At critical moments, the CPC's own debates were shaped by Lenin's theoretical insights on several key points, but two in particular are especially relevant, namely:

a] Identifying the specific socio-economic features of the country in transition
b] Optimising the synergy between the productive forces and the relations of productions

a] Specific features of transition in Russia and China

The key question for socialists in advanced capitalist societies is to develop revolutionary strategies to overthrow the capitalist system and replace it with socialism. The process of how to successfully make this transition from capitalism to socialism has so far remained elusive, despite the high level of economic development (productive forces) and the relatively streamlined class structures (a key element of the relations of production) in these countries. Both the Russian and Chinese revolutions occurred in societies with extremely weak and undeveloped capitalist economies (China much more so than the European territories of the Russian empire) and with significant vestiges of pre-capitalist communities and modes of production.

Lenin was acutely aware that the Soviet transition "to socialism" was not simply "from capitalism".

> No one, I think, in studying the question of the economic system of Russia, has denied its transitional character. Nor, I think, has any Communist denied that the term Soviet Socialist Republic implies the determination of the Soviet

THE 'PRIMARY STAGE OF SOCIALISM' IN HISTORICAL CONTEXT

> power to achieve the transition to socialism, and not that the existing economic system is recognised as a socialist order.
>
> But what does the word "transition" mean? Does it not mean, as applied to an economy, that the present system contains elements, particles, fragments of both capitalism and socialism? Everyone will admit that it does. But not all who admit this take the trouble to consider what elements actually constitute the various socio-economic structures that exist in Russia at the present time. And this is the crux of the question.
>
> Let us enumerate these elements:
> (1) patriarchal, i.e., to a considerable extent natural, peasant farming;
> (2) small commodity production (this includes the majority of those peasants who sell their grain);
> (3) private capitalism;
> (4) state capitalism;
> (5) socialism.
>
> Russia is so vast and so varied that all these different types of socio-economic structures are intermingled. This is what constitutes the specific feature of the situation."[7]

In a similar vein, Mao Zedong suggested that there were seven forms of socio-economic structures on the territory of the young People's Republic, four major ones and three others in largely minority areas, the latter further complicating the solution of even the democratic tasks of the Chinese revolution, such as land reform, women's liberation and so on.

Speaking in 1954, Mao noted:

> Article 5 of our Draft Constitution states that four forms of ownership of the means of production exist in the People's Republic of China ['state ownership, that is, ownership by the whole people; co-operative ownership, that is, collective ownership by the working masses; ownership by individual working people; and capitalist ownership.']. In fact, there are other forms of ownership in our minority nationality areas. Does primitive communal ownership still exist in our country? I'm afraid it does among some minority nationalities. Similarly, slave ownership and feudal ownership still exist. From a contemporary standpoint the

slave system, the feudal system and the capitalist system are all bad, but historically they were more progressive than the primitive communal system. These systems were progressive at first but not later on and were therefore supplanted in their turn. Article 70 of our Draft Constitution stipulates that the minority nationality areas "may, in the light of the political, economic and cultural characteristics of the nationality or nationalities in a given area, make regulations on the exercise of autonomy as well as specific regulations". All these are instances of the integration of principle and flexibility.[8]

In short, People's China's starting point in 1949 (see Jenny Clegg's chapter for further detail) was not that of a society emerging from the womb of an advanced or 'pure' capitalism but rather one with multiple pre-capitalist forms. The imprints of China's birthmarks and length and frequency of its birth pangs were naturally of a corresponding order.

b] Dialectics of the forces and relations of productions
Marxism insists that each specific society develops through the dialectical relationship between the forces of production and the relations of production. The latter includes forms of property ownership but also the many levels of technical and managerial relations between those involved in any given mode of production.

Lenin thought that in certain circumstances capitalism could be used to accelerate the socialisation and integration of the scattered means of production as well as to modernise them. Writing in 1921, he suggested Soviet power could guide and direct the capitalist sector of the economy not by negatively suppressing and restricting it but by steering it in the course charted by the socialist state.

> Over the next few years we must learn to think of the intermediary links that can facilitate the transition from patriarchalism and small production to socialism. "We" continue saying now and again that "capitalism is a bane and socialism is a boon". But such an argument is wrong, because it fails to take into account the aggregate of the existing economic forms and singles out only two of them.
>
> Capitalism is a bane compared with socialism. Capitalism is a boon compared with medievalism, small production, and the evils of bureaucracy which spring from the dispersal of the small producers. Inasmuch as we are as yet unable to pass directly from small production to socialism, some capitalism is inevitable as the elemental product of small production

and exchange; so that we must utilise capitalism (particularly by directing it into the channels of state capitalism) as the intermediary link between small production and socialism, as a means, a path, and a method of increasing the productive forces.[9]

While acknowledging the backwardness of Russia's economic and cultural development, which made the immediate achievement of socialism possible, Lenin concluded that it was perfectly feasible to gradually develop the productive forces to a point where the beginnings of a socialist society could be built.

> If a definite level of culture is required for the building of socialism (although nobody can say just what that definite "level of culture" is, for it differs in every Western European country), why cannot we begin by first achieving the prerequisites for that definite level of culture in a revolutionary way, and then, with the aid of the workers' and peasants' government and Soviet system, proceed to overtake the other nations?
>
> ... Our European philistines never even dream that the subsequent revolutions in Oriental countries, which possess much vaster populations in a much vaster diversity of social conditions, will undoubtedly display even greater distinctions than the Russian Revolution.[10]

This was a particularly significant insight for the CPC. Lenin viewed the Russian and even more so foreign capitalists as fundamentally hostile to Soviet development, yet they both had their uses. For the CPC, applying the concept of New Democracy, there was a specific stratum of the Chinese capitalist class – the national bourgeoisie – which, while a temporary and irresolute political ally against imperialism and feudalism, also possessed sufficient resources, as well as economic self-interest, to be harnessed in expanding the productive forces essential for China's reconstruction.[11] (Again see Jenny Clegg's chapter).

3] Summing up Soviet socialism – from Stalin to Gorbachev

In its early years the CPC experienced two trends in approaches to the Soviet Union, which could be considered a contest between imitation and emulation. The first saw the Soviet experience as a template into which Chinese reality had to be fitted. This approach was adopted by a number of CPC leaders in the 1920s and 30s in particular and was also reinforced at times by directions or advice from the Communist International.[12]

However, the second trend sifted the Soviet experience more selectively, adapting certain features to the specifics of China. The worker-peasant alliance was common to both Chinese and Soviet experiences, for example, but the recognition of China's semi-feudal economy and its semi-colonial status, with some territories under direct foreign imperialist occupation, allowed China's worker-peasant coalition to serve as a nucleus for broader anti-feudal and anti-imperialist alliances with other classes and strata.

The CPC made public its differences over a number of these historical issues in 1956. The CPC responded to the public resolutions of the 20th Congress of the CPSU and the so-called "Secret Speech" in which Soviet leader Nikita Khrushchev had vehemently denounced Stalin. Although not published in the Soviet Union, the CPC was given a copy of the speech's contents. The CPC response *On the Historical Experience of the Dictatorship of the Proletariat* was nuanced and balanced, seeking to place Stalin's errors and abuses in a wider historical and material context that went beyond Khrushchev's focus on the 'cult of personality'. It rejected a wholesale repudiation of Stalin, insisting that his leadership was also responsible for tremendous achievements, such as industrialisation and the defeat of Nazism. The CPC defended Stalin as "an outstanding Marxist-Leninist fighter" who had nonetheless made serious errors on a whole host of questions, from arbitrary use of repression to chauvinist relations with foreign socialist countries,[13] but one criticism that was most relevant to China's situation was the belief that Stalin had "failed to pay proper attention to the further development of agriculture and the material welfare of the peasantry".

Among other points, the CPC urged the recognition that:

> Socialist society also develops through contradictions
> between the productive forces and the relations of production.
> In a socialist or communist society, technical innovations and
> improvement in the social system inevitably continue to take
> place; otherwise the development of society would come to a
> standstill and society could no longer advance.[14]

This theme was taken up by Mao the same month in a speech *On the Ten Major Relationships*, which applied this approach to the specifics of China's development. Later in 1956, serious disturbances erupted in Poland (June) and an armed rising in Hungary (October). This led to a second statement published in late December, *More On the Historical Experience of the Dictatorship of the Proletariat*, which insisted on the need to distinguish between contradictions among the people and contradictions between the people and the enemy. This second statement clearly reflected concerns that anti-socialist forces were gaining momentum and that right-wing revisionism, identified at this point with the Yugoslavs, was playing into their hands. Mao developed these points with a major speech in early 1957, *On the Correct Handling of Contradictions Among the People*.

However, relations between the two major socialist states gradually deteriorated with Khrushchev's increasingly erratic and high-handed leadership treating the Chinese side with disdain and, on the other, the CPC's criticisms of the Soviet Union reflecting the growing influence of exaggerated leftist analysis, culminating not only in the refusal to regard the USSR as a socialist state but even in the 1969 words of Lin Biao that it had become "a dark fascist state under the dictatorship of the bourgeoisie".

After the Cultural Revolution, however, in the context of far greater political stability, the Soviet socialist experience provided a renewed source of research. In two fascinating works covering the 1970s to the mid-1980s, Gilbert Rozman contrasted Soviet analyses of China with Chinese perspectives on the Soviet Union.[15] His work showed that while the Brezhnev period was ideologically stagnant, Chinese scholars and advisers in the post-Cultural Revolution era were quick to take advantage of greater intellectual freedom by delving deeper into Soviet history. This focused not only on the role of Lenin, Stalin and Khrushchev, and the contradictions of existing Soviet society but also made serious explorations into the life and work of controversial historical figures such as Leon Trotsky and especially Nikolai Bukharin. This contrasted with the restrictions on these topics faced by their Soviet counterparts.

Rozman showed that Chinese studies of the Soviet economy, from War Communism through to the New Economic Policy and then collectivisation and industrialisation, were considered particularly important, as were considerations of the contemporary functioning of more market-oriented European socialist states, such as Hungary and Yugoslavia. However, the chief criterion was not to find any foreign model to copy but to learn from international experience and extract relevant elements which could be adapted to China. One concept that was almost universally rejected was the idea that the Soviet Union represented a form of "developed socialism". In 1961, during the Khrushchev period, the CPSU had adopted a programme that predicted that the USSR would begin the transition from socialism to full communism by 1980. This utopian idea was gradually dropped in favour of the concept of "developed socialism" during the Brezhnev era, however this too exaggerated the productivity and efficiency levels of the Soviet economy.

These debates had the positive effect of acting as a foil to reframe discussions about China's own "undeveloped" status, highlighting the dangers of following policies that did not accord with the actual stage of development.

The collapse of the Soviet Union, which occurred around the time of warming relations between Beijing and Moscow, provided a final impulse for reconsidering not only the economic, but political and ideological crises that China seeks to avoid.[16]

4] Reform and Opening Up – Socialism Defended and Reassessed

The term 'primary stage of socialism' appeared publicly at the 13th CPC congress in 1987, however the concept if not the wording was already in circulation a decade before. The first key turning point was the 3rd Plenary of the 11th Central Committee held in December 1978, which called for "changes in the relations of production and the superstructure, methods of management, form of activity and ways of thinking which do not accord with the development of the forces of production".[17] On the 30th anniversary of the founding of the PRC a year later, Ye Jianying noted that China was a "still a developing socialist country. Our socialist system has to be improved and our economy and culture are still under-developed", the socialist system was still in its 'infancy' and there were still birthmarks from the heritage of old feudal society.[18]

Insisting that socialism must prove itself in practice, two years before the 13th congress Deng Xiaoping noted that:

> In order to realise communism, we have to accomplish the tasks set in the socialist stage. They are legion, but the fundamental one is to develop the productive forces so as to demonstrate the superiority of socialism over capitalism and provide the material basis for communism. For a long time we neglected the development of the productive forces of the socialist society. From 1957 on they grew at a snail's pace. In the countryside, after ten years – that is, in 1966 – the peasants' income had risen only very slightly. Although peasants in some areas were better off, those in many other areas still lived in poverty. Of course, even that was progress, compared with the old days. Still, it was far from a socialist standard of living.[19]

Nonetheless, a number of questions remain to be worked out in practice. A particular source of concern to many socialists outside China is the existence of new capitalist strata. So far, these strata have thrived economically due to their adherence to the political guardrails set by the CPC and central government. China's communists can after all draw upon their considerable experience of working with the old national bourgeoisie and their peaceful buyout. China has modernised its state-owned sector and has adopted a multi-tier approach to ownership in the private sector. One recent innovation is the creation of "special management shares" which allow minority stakes to control large conglomerates, ensuring they follow overall national development plans and engage in productive not parasitic enterprise. This has been used to rein in certain sectors, such as technology, where state investment firms become shareholders.[20] This is an innovation that derives directly from the concept of the socialist market economy that sees public ownership as the economic mainstay. This maintains the socialist character of China but in ways that are historically unprecedented, intertwining forms of traditionally discrete socialist, state-capitalist and private ownerships into an integrated whole.

5] Entering the New Era

While the primary contradiction of Chinese society is still the development of the productive forces, an important distinction was introduced by Xi Jinping in 2017, namely that China's greatest challenge was to transform the economy by moving from the first phase of rapid quantitative growth to a stage of high-quality development. Particular attention is being given to the "new high-quality productive forces", such as in the digital and green economic sectors, as a means to overcome the imbalances of the previous few decades, the changing priorities of the Chinese population and the new challenges of international competition.

Two landmark goals, called the Two Centenaries, stand out. The first (accomplished in 2021, marking 100 years since the foundation of the CPC) was to achieve "a moderately prosperous society in all respects"; in monetary terms this meant doubling China's economy and citizens' disposable income between 2010 and 2020. The second centenary goal is to construct "a great modern socialist country in all respects by 2049", the 100th anniversary of the founding of People's China, with a midway target in 2035 that aims to double China's economy from its 2020 level.

Economist Justin Yifu Lin has estimated that:

> per capita GDP in China will reach half of that of the US by 2049. Some developed Chinese municipalities and provinces like Beijing, Shanghai, Zhejiang province and Guangdong province will be at the same level as the US in terms of GDP per capita, industries and the level of technology.[21]

The goal is not solely economic; the aim is to carry out modernisation in five fields: modernisation of a huge population, common prosperity for all, material and cultural-ethical advance, harmony between humanity and nature, and peaceful development.[22]

The last point, of course, is not solely in the hands of China but will depend on cooperation rather than confrontation dominating in international relations. We can therefore expect repeated attempts by the United States and others to block or undermine both China's development and its socialist path since the two are inextricably linked.

The concept of the primary stage of socialism has served China well, avoiding both the errors of the "rash advances" of the past and the disastrous consequences of capitalist restoration on the other. How many more stages China will need to fully complete its socialist tasks is impossible to say. Cheng Enfu argues convincingly for the existence of three main phases – primary, intermediary and advanced – but how many subsidiary stages will emerge cannot reasonably be predicted. We cannot forecast the precise timeline for these stages, nor can we foresee the effects of the much-needed revival of a wider international socialist community.[23]

Marxists internationally should be engaging more actively in studying and learning from China not only to absorb key lessons from the most important socialist project of the contemporary world but also to ensure the continuing development of Marxism itself.

NOTES

All online content accessed 10 September 2024.

1. CPC Constitution, General Program, p5. Online: https://english.www.gov.cn/news/topnews/202210/26/content_WS635921cdc6d0a757729e1cd4.html
2. Marx's *Grundrisse* (1857-58) and Engels' *Origin of the Family, Private Property and the State* (1884), are the two best-known examples.
3. *The Civil War in France*, 1891 Introduction by Frederick Engels 'On the 20th Anniversary of the Paris Commune'. Online: https://www.marxists.org/archive/marx/works/1871/civil-war-france/postscript.htm
4. Musto, Marcello 'The Experience of the Paris Commune and Marx's Reflections on Communism', Chapter from Marcello Musto (Ed.), *Rethinking Alternatives with Marx: Economy, Ecology and Migration*, Palgrave Macmillan, 2021, pp. 263-284. Online: https://marcellomusto.org/experience-of-the-paris-commune/
5. Marx, Karl *Critique of the Gotha Programme (1875)*. Online: https://www.marxists.org/archive/marx/works/1875/gotha/ch01.htm
6. Ibid.
7. 'The Tax in Kind', Lenin 1921, Collected Works, Vol 32. Online: https://www.marxists.org/archive/lenin/works/1921/apr/21.htm
8. Mao Zedong, 'On the Draft Constitution of the People's Republic of China' June 14, 1954, *Selected Works* Vol 5. Online: https://www.marxists.org/reference/archive/mao/selected-works/volume-5/mswv5_37.htm
9. Lenin, 'The Tax in Kind', 1921. Online at https://www.marxists.org/archive/lenin/works/1921/apr/21.htm
10. Lenin 'Our Revolution' (final excerpt added 16 January, 1923). Online: https://www.marxists.org/archive/lenin/works/1923/jan/16.htm
11. Depending on the situation, Mao advocated even wider temporary class alliances, see *On the Question of the National Bourgeoisie and the Enlightened Gentry* (March 1, 1948). Online: https://www.marxists.org/reference/archive/mao/selected-works/volume-4/index.htm
12. For a recent discussion see Cheng, Enfu & Yang, Jun. 'The Chinese Revolution and the Communist International'. *Third World Quarterly*, 41(8). (2020)
13. 'On the Historical Experience of the Dictatorship of the Proletariat', 5 April, 1956, *Renmin Ribao*. Online: https://www.marxists.org/history/international/comintern/sino-soviet-split/cpc/hedp.htm It says of Stalin's errors that he "broadened the scope of the suppression of counter-revolution; he lacked the necessary vigilance on the eve of the anti-fascist war; he failed to pay proper attention

to the further development of agriculture and the material welfare of the peasantry; he gave certain wrong advice on the international communist movement, and, in particular, made a wrong decision on the question of Yugoslavia. On these issues, Stalin fell victim to subjectivism and one-sidedness, and divorced himself from objective reality and from the masses."
An exhaustive overview of recent Chinese debates on Stalin can be found in *New Research on Stalin's Socialism Thought: A Historical and Realistic Analysis*. Edited by Gu Hailiang, Canut Publishers (2017).

14 Ibid.
15 See Gilbert Rozman: *A Mirror for Socialism – Soviet Criticisms of China*, Princeton University Press (1986); *The Chinese Debate about Soviet Socialism, 1978–1985*, Princeton University Press (1987).
16 An updated survey of recent Chinese research on Soviet history, driven by the need to identify the specific causes of the Soviet Union's collapse, can be found in Zuo Fengrong 'A Review of Chinese Scholarship on the Collapse of the Soviet Union', originally published in *Issues of Contemporary World Socialism* (Beijing), English translation by CSIS. PDF downloaded from https://interpret.csis.org/translations/a-review-of-chinese-scholarship-on-the-collapse-of-the-soviet-union/
17 Plenum communique quoted in *A Concise History of the Communist Party of China*, edited by Hu Sheng, Beijing 1994, page 753.
18 'Comrade Ye Jinyang's Speech at the Meeting in Celebration of the 30th anniversary of the Founding of the People's Republic of China', *Beijing Review* no 40, 5 October 1979.
19 Deng Xiaoping 'Reform Is the Only Way For China to Develop Its Productive Forces' 1985. Online: https://www.marxists.org/reference/archive/deng-xiaoping/1985/112.htm
20 See 'China moves to take "golden shares" in Alibaba and Tencent units'. Ryan McMorrow, Qianer Liu, Cheng Leng, *Financial Times*, January 13, 2023. Online https://www.ft.com/content/65e60815-c5a0-4c4a-bcec-4af0f76462de
21 'Goal 2049: Modern, strong nation despite hurdles', Justin Yifu Lin, *China Daily*, 23 August 2021. Online: https://global.chinadaily.com.cn/a/202108/23/WS6122f7b0a310efa1bd66a62c.html
22 See 'Five Characteristics of Chinese Modernization', Qu Qingshan. Source: English Edition of *Qiushi Journal*, 14 November 2023. Online http://en.qstheory.cn/2023-11/14/c_938533.htm
23 Cheng Enfu. 'On the Three Stages in the Development of Socialism'. *Science & Society*. 86. 159-181. (2022)

6

China's socialist democracy

Roland Boer

The key to understanding socialist democracy – and thus China's socialist democracy – is as follows: socialist democracy strengthens the leadership of the Communist Party, and the leadership of the Communist Party strengthens socialist democracy.

Explaining this core point requires consideration of the relation between theory and practice, democracy and Party leadership, democratic centralism, and the statutory processes that mediate the relation between democracy and Party leadership.

Practice and Theory

To return to the opening sentence concerning the key to understanding China's socialist democracy, the reason for beginning with this dialectical point is twofold: first, the following explication of China's socialist democracy takes a deliberately theoretical and indeed philosophical approach; second, this by now well-developed theory has arisen from and interacted with more than a century of the actual practice of socialist governance, from the time of the October Revolution in 1917 until today in socialist countries. Let me say a little more about each point, beginning with the second.

The practice of socialist governance begins from the moment a Communist Party gains power through a proletarian revolution. All that went before becomes theoretical reflection awaiting practice, which can either verify the theory or lead to revisions in light of testing on the ground. For example, Engels's principles of socialist governance (Boer 2021a) or Lenin's *State and Revolution* (1917) contain proposals that came before socialism in power.

However insightful they may be, the principles and theories proposed still needed to be tested in the furnace of revolution and the initial steps in governance. Far more interesting are the theoretical developments that came through a long tradition of trial, error, testing anew, and reformulation. For a reader interested in the detail of this history, allow me to refer to a work entitled *Socialism In Power: On the History and Theory of Socialist Governance* (Boer 2023).

As for the importance of philosophy, the reason for taking this approach is that while one may find more and more works available in English that explain the practices of socialist governance in China, treatments of the philosophical underpinnings remain somewhat sparse. Thus, it is relatively easy to find explanations of the workings of China's electoral system, with the five levels of people's congresses, qualifications for candidates, numbers of candidates needed for an election, eligibility for voting, statistics on participation, and so on. The same applies to the integrated consultative democracy, including grassroots democratic practices, legislative contact points, and the active roles of the nine political parties, 55 minority nationalities, religious groups, important political personages, and so on. Further, an increasing number of works are now available in English (primarily through the active translation and publication program with Springer and the Chinese Academy of Social Sciences) on the development of China's distinct socialist legal system and the rule of law. An interested reader is encouraged to pursue such works by some of China's leading specialists so as to gain a comprehensive understanding of how the system has developed, how it works, and what the plans are for further development and strengthening.

Democracy and Party Leadership

To return to the initial dialectical point. Let us put this now in terms of two principles: China upholds the leadership of the Communist Party and the people as centre, as masters of the country. To a reader brought up a Western context, these may seem like two opposite poles: they might think that you can have either the people as masters of the country or the leadership of the Communist Party, but not both. It may take some time for a reader to understand what is at stake here, but if you want to understand China's socialist governance you must understand this point. To explain:

First, this is a core philosophical point, or more precisely a dialectical point. Thus, it is not a case of either-or, but both-and: both the leadership of the Communist Party and the people as masters of the country. This dialectical tendency runs deep in the Chinese cultural tradition and is manifested at so many levels, from the food one eats, through town planning, to assumptions concerning politics. It also resonates deeply with the Marxist tradition, which is a dialectical materialist tradition – one of the major reasons Marxism took root in China.[1]

Second, a key breakthrough in the history of socialist governance was the realisation that you cannot have a socialist political system without the leadership of the Communist Party. This reality became apparent in the Soviet Union and has become a staple of socialist democracy ever since. We may put it this way: without the leadership of the Communist Party you do not have a socialist political system, that is, you do not have socialist democracy. The leadership of the Communist Party is a defining feature of socialist democracy.

Third, the people as masters of the country, or a people-centred approach. On this matter, a Western reader may assume a framework of the "sovereignty of the people," which arose in the struggle with the *ancien regime* in Europe (think of the French revolutions and those that followed) and saw – as the story goes – a transfer of sovereignty from a monarch and to the people. A Marxist approach is quite distinct: as the representative and vanguard of the vast majority – urban and rural workers – a Communist Party embodies the democratic choice of the people through the revolutionary process of taking power and beginning on the long road of socialist construction. This process of construction is by and for the vast majority, seeking to lift everyone out of poverty and attain common prosperity.

One may object: are these not simply different concepts of "popular sovereignty," expressions of the "will of the people"? Here we broach an important topic concerning democratic systems. We may distinguish between two approaches. To begin with, it may be argued that there is no "one size fits all" in terms of political systems, that each arises from and is appropriate to the specific history, culture, and society of a region or a country. Thus, the imposition of a Western capitalist political system – which has its own history and particularities – on other parts of the world means a distinctly bad fit, leading to instability and chaos. While this comparative point has some merit, it takes us only so far. More interesting is the qualitative question: are there more genuine forms of democracy, forms that more truly express the will of the people? From my research over the last decade, it has become very clear that China's socialist democracy is already more mature, robust, substantive and inclusive than any type you will find elsewhere.

Let me put it this way: three of the "core socialist values" are democracy, equality, and freedom. A superficial reading might equate these with Western capitalist concepts, but this would constitute a profound mistake. Why? For the Marxist tradition, democracy, equality, and freedom have a qualitatively distinct meaning. They apply to the vast majority: workers, peasants-farmers, and in formerly colonised countries the Indigenous peoples. Ultimately, this is a question of qualitative difference, since within socialism they have a more genuine meaning. To explain: Chinese scholars often refer to Marx's *Economic Manuscripts of 1857-1858*, where he proposes that the development of human society goes through three communal stages:

first, the pre-capitalist era was based on "relations of human dependence," that is, the "naturally evolved community"; the second is capitalist society based on "dependence mediated by things," that is, a false or "illusory community"; the third is communist society based on "individual all-round development," that is, the true or "real community" in which "individuals attain their freedom in and through their association" (Marx 1858, 95, 415, 420).[2] In their works, Marx and Engels often used the "real community" and the "free development of each is the condition for the free development of all" to refer to the future communist society (Marx and Engels 1848, 506). This is the framework for understanding the meanings of democracy, freedom, and equality. In a capitalist society, these values are illusory and lack substance. By contrast, from a Marxist perspective democracy, freedom, and equality have a genuine and substantive meaning.

Democratic Centralism and Statutory Processes

The question remains: how does substantive or whole-process people's democracy relate to the leadership of the Communist Party? Two inter-related points need to be made here, concerning democratic centralism and the statutory procedures.

As for democratic centralism, I have elsewhere dealt at some length with its history, from its initial identification by the Bolsheviks in 1904-1905 until today (Boer 2021b, 248–57). In light of this history, we may identify two levels: democratic centralism in terms of the Party's own functioning; and democratic centralism for country-wide governance. While the former has become an established practice of Communist Parties since the early twentieth century, the long-standing problem has concerned the way to make democratic centralism work for country-wide governance.

In the Chinese context, the effort began with Deng Xiaoping's (1986, 177) initial emphasis that the CPC's "functions should be separated from those of the government." In other words, the government of the country, embodied in the many levels of people's congresses and people's political consultative conferences, would become separated from the role of the CPC. Deng was responding to the chaotic leftist deviation of the "Cultural Revolution" when the will of one person was taken as law – known as "rule of a person." While Jiang Zemin (2002, 553) would take this a step further in emphasising the crucial role of a socialist rule of law as the way to ensure the mutual role of CPC leadership and socialist democracy, it would be Hu Jintao who spelled out exactly what this means. One of Hu Jintao's most important points was that the whole structure of socialist democracy would ensure that "the Party's proposals become the will of the country through statutory procedures" (Hu 2007, 13; see also 2012, 17). How so? As Hu put it in 2012, the "basic strategy by which the party leads the people in governing the country is through governing the country according to law" (Hu 2012, 9).

It would fall to Xi Jinping to clarify that these processes are required for democratic centralism to work at a country-wide level. Xi Jinping also stresses the need to improve even more the CPC's indirect leadership through the legal or statutory procedures of rule of law governance (Xi 2012, 142; 2015, 17; 2019, 3). When the Party's policies become state laws, "the implementation of the law is the implementation of the Party's will, and the implementation of the Party's policies is to act in accordance with the law" (Xi 2015, 18). All of this entails that the organs of state power are independent, proactive, and responsible in terms of adhering to the constitution and relevant laws.

The explicit connection with democratic centralism was already made a decade ago:

> Adhering to the principle of democratic centralism, the system of state power and the standards of actions defined in the constitution, we should exercise state power through the people's congresses, ensure that decision-making power, executive power, and oversight power function independently but are coordinated with each other, ensure that government agencies exercise their power and perform their duties in accordance with statutory mandates and procedures, and ensure that government agencies organise all undertakings concertedly and effectively (Xi 2012, 139).

Later in the same text, Xi (2012, 142) speaks of democratic centralism in terms of the "foundational" way of "exercising power according to law" and "governing the country according to law." This text comes very early in the time of the Eighteenth Central Committee, and the speech in question was initially delivered in 2012 at a thirtieth anniversary celebration of the 1982 constitution. From 2012 until today, the Central Committee with Xi Jinping at its core has been focused on strengthening adherence to the constitution, on developing China's democratic system, and on ensuring the leadership of the Communist Party. All of this may be described as democratic centralism, which relies on the reality that the "authority of both Party and state" are distinct (Xi 2015, 20; 2017, 28).

The above summarises a rather complex development, but let me quote Ma Yide's (2017, 31) description of the basic logic of China's system of governance:

> First, the Party's leadership is political leadership, and the Party's views are a combination of historical and practical legitimacy based on multi-party cooperation and political consultation. Second, the Party's views, which have solid legitimacy, are transformed into the will of the state through

people's congresses, and the concrete expression of the will of the state is democratic legislation. During this process, the people re-examine and substantiate the Party's views through the system of people's congresses. Third, as the legal procedure for transforming the will of the Party, democratic legislation constitutes the basis for governing the country according to law, and is the governance basis for the direct links between the modern state and citizens. Fourth, the leadership of the Party should advance with the times through consultations between the Party and the masses and social consultation, thereby entering the logical chain of direct governance consisting of legitimisation of the Party's views and their transformation into the will of the state and thence into the rule of law, thus successfully coordinating state governance and social development.

Conclusion

In this relatively brief exposition, I have attempted to provide some philosophical background to the core feature of China's socialist democracy: the full system of socialist democracy does not weaken but strengthens the CPC's leadership; conversely, only through the CPC's leadership are the institutions of socialist democracy strengthened. In other words, the leadership of the Communist Party ensures that the people are masters of the country, and the robust exercise of socialist democracy ensures that the Communist Party continues its role of legitimate leadership. This analysis has entailed an initial discussion of practice and theory, the two aspects of democracy and Party leadership, and the treatment of democratic centralism and the crucial role of statutory procedures that ensure that the will of the Party and the people align with one another.

To finish with the question of evaluation and quality. For the past few years, Chinese scholars have been engaged in detailed analysis of China's comprehensive and integrated system of governance, which is described as an "interlocking chain" of elections, consultation, decision-making, management, and supervision – in relation to state, economic, social, and cultural affairs (Kuai 2021, 73–75; Cheng 2022; Li 2022, 28). In other words, this democracy is "full-chain, all-dimensional, and all-encompassing," and thereby "the most extensive, authentic, and effective socialist democracy" (Xi 2022, 5).

REFERENCES

Boer, Roland. 2021a. *Friedrich Engels and the Foundations of Socialist Governance*. Singapore: Springer.
———. 2021b. *Socialism with Chinese Characteristics: A Guide for Foreigners*. Singapore: Springer.
———. 2023. *Socialism in Power: On the History and Theory of Socialist Governance*. Singapore: Springer.
Cheng, Tongshun. 2022. "The Systemic Organisation, Democratic Practice, and Governance Effectiveness of Whole-Process People's Democracy." *Studies on Party and Governance* 2022 (2): 77–83. (In Chinese.)
Deng, Xiaoping. 1986. "On Reform of the Political Structure (September–November 1986)". In *Selected Works of Deng Xiaoping*, Vol. 3:176–80. Beijing: People's Publishing House, 2008. (In Chinese.)
Hu, Jintao. 2007. *Hold High the Great Banner of Socialism with Chinese Characteristics and Strive for New Victories in Building a Moderately Prosperous Society in all Respects. Report to the Seventeenth National Congress of the Communist Party of China on 15 October, 2007*. Beijing: People's Publishing House. (In Chinese.)
———. 2012. *Firmly March on the Path of Socialism with Chinese Characteristics and Strive to Complete the Building of a Moderately Prosperous Society in All Respects. Report to the Eighteenth National Congress of the Communist Party of China on 8 November, 2012*. Beijing: People's Publishing House. (In Chinese.)
Jiang, Zemin. 2002. "Build a Moderately Prosperous Society in All Respects and Open Up New Prospects for the Cause of Socialism with Chinese Characteristics. Report to the Sixteenth National Congress of the Communist Party of China on 8 November, 2002." In *The Selected Works of Jiang Zemin*, Vol. 3:528–75. Beijing: People's Publishing House, 2006. (In Chinese).
Kuai, Zhengming. 2021. "The Contribution of Whole-Process People's Democracy to Human Political Civilisation." *Studies in Marxism* 2021 (9): 71–78. (In Chinese.)
Li, Zhong. 2022. "On the Systemic and Legal Transformations of Whole Process People's Democracy." *Journal of Northwestern University (Philosophy and Social Sciences Edition)* 2022 (1): 27–36.
Lenin, V. I. 1917. "The State and Revolution: The Marxist Theory of the State and the Tasks of the Proletariat in the Revolution (1917)". In *Collected Works*, Vol. 25:385–497. Moscow: Progress Publishers, 1964.
Ma, Yide. 2017. "The Role of Consultative Democracy under the Constitutional Framework and the Associated Rule of Law". *Social Sciences in China* 38 (2): 21–38.
Marx, Karl. 1858. "Economic Manuscripts of 1857-58 (First Version of Capital) [Grundrisse]". In *Marx and Engels Collected Works*. Vol. 28. Moscow:

Progress Publishers, 1986.

Marx, Karl, and Friedrich Engels. 1846. "The German Ideology: Critique of Modern German Philosophy according to Its Representatives Feuerbach, B. Bauer and Stirner, and of German Socialism according to Its Various Prophets". In *Marx and Engels Collected Works*, Vol. 5:19–539. Moscow: Progress Publishers, 1976.

———. 1848. "The Manifesto of the Communist Party". In *Marx and Engels Collected Works*, Vol. 6:477–519. Moscow: Progress Publishers, 1976.

Xi, Jinping. 2012. "Commemorate the 30th Anniversary of the Promulgation and Implementation of the Current Constitution (4 December, 2012)". In *The Governance of China*, Vol. 1:135–43. Beijing: Foreign Languages Press, 2014.

———. 2015. *On Comprehensively Governing the Country According to Law*. Beijing: Central Literary Publishing House. (In Chinese.)

———. 2017. "The Leadership of the Communist Party of China is the Most Essential Characteristic of Socialism with Chinese Characteristics (5 September 2014 – 13 February, 2017)". In *The Governance of China*, Vol. 2:28–30. Beijing: Foreign Languages Press, 2017. (In Chinese.)

———. 2019. "Strengthen the Party's Leadership Through Comprehensively Governing the Country According to Law (24 August, 2018)". *Qiushi* 2019 (4): 1–4. (In Chinese.)

———. "Speech at a Working Conference of the National People's Congress (13 October, 2021). *Qiushi* 2022 (5): 1–5.

NOTES

1. I will not reiterate here the history of this engagement, from developments in the Soviet Union, through the immensely creative period in China's Yan'an under the leadership of Mao Zedong in the second half of the 1930s, to the China of today.
2. The phrases "illusory community," "real community," and "individuals attain their freedom in and through their association" come from *The German Ideology* (Marx and Engels 1846, 46, 78).

THIS PAGE INTENTIONALLY LEFT BLANK

7

Common prosperity

Michael Dunford

Common prosperity and prosperity are relative concepts. In the case of China, the Tang, Yuan, Song, Ming and early Qing Dynasty were all prosperous. Indeed China was one of the richest countries in the world until it was semi-colonised in the mid-nineteenth century and subsequently invaded by a succession of foreign powers, even though the level of material wealth fell far short of that of contemporary societies. Up until the first industrial revolution the average differences in relative prosperity of different parts of the world were not especially large. After the first industrial revolution, however, average differences in the degree of national and regional prosperity increased sharply. As differences in relative prosperity increased, each country judged whether it was rich or poor and strong or weak by comparing itself with the most advanced countries. Sometimes these judgements are interpreted as reflecting differences in the degree of modernisation (as if there were only one path). Again the concept is a relative one.

While countries and different parts of the world judge whether they are prosperous or not by comparing themselves in average terms with other parts of the world, individuals and groups judge their own degree of prosperity in relative terms by comparing it with those of others. In *Wage Labour and Capital,* Marx pointed out that:

> A house may be large or small; as long as the surrounding houses are equally small it satisfies all social demands for a

> dwelling. But let a palace arise beside the little house, and it shrinks from a little house to a hut. The little house shows now that its owner has only very slight or no demands to make; and however high it may shoot up in the course of civilization, if the neighbouring palace grows to an equal or even greater extent, the occupant of the relatively small house will feel more and more uncomfortable, dissatisfied and cramped within its four walls.(Marx, 1952 [1891, 1847], p. 41)

Common or shared prosperity refers to a situation in which the prosperity of everyone increases and prosperity is shared. For this reason, good indices of the extent to which prosperity is common or shared are the degrees of inequality and of social polarisation. It does not mean absolute equality, but it does mean that differences are not large and that they do not increase.

As such common prosperity is a socialist concept. Capitalism not only opened up immense disparities between countries (initially countries that industrialised and urbanised and those that did not and were colonised or otherwise dominated by industrial powers) but also immense inequalities among their inhabitants. Governments in capitalist countries may seek to limit these differences to different degrees at different times. At the root of social inequalities however are the foundational principles of capitalist modes of production: the establishment of private property in land and the means of production and their self-reinforcing concentration in a few hands along with the dispossession and proletarianisation of the great majority of the population, converted into a dependent wage-earning class.

These considerations help one understand why Deng Xiaoping (Deng, 1999) repeatedly argued that common prosperity is one of the two main characteristics of socialism, and that the second main characteristic is the public ownership of economic assets. Deng defined common prosperity as the avoidance of social polarisation (again a relative concept referring to the absence of wide differences in the degree of prosperity of different groups and different individuals), and he insisted that the existence of public property and collective assets could prevent social polarisation. In that situation earnings depend largely on wage income (differing as wages reflect different contributions): China adheres to the principle of 'distribution according to labour as the main body'. At the same time public ownership limits the possibilities of private individuals securing very high incomes as a result of personal possession/ownership of means of production and the exploitation of labour by capital (Wèi, 2021)shíxiàn gòngtóng fùyù - only public ownership can eliminate polarization and achieve common prosperity] as well, one might add, of personal appropriation of rent and interest from privately owned real estate and financial capital.

In China the concept of common prosperity was first used in 1953 as a central goal of the collective leadership of the Communist Party of China

(CPC) and the Chinese government (Michael Dunford, 2022; Tang, 2023). At that time the immediate aim was to establish rural production cooperatives. This measure would help generate an investible surplus and provide market outlets for farm equipment and simple consumer goods, contributing significantly to the new China's early economic progress. At the same time it helped improve the conditions of the agricultural population in ways in which everyone would benefit.

Until the early 1970s China confronted United States embargoes. From the late 1950s until the 1980s it also had to deal with a conflictual relationship with the Soviet Union. In the 1960s these threats diverted much of China's resources to Third Front development and the transfer of strategic industries to places less vulnerable to Soviet and US aggression. And yet in these difficult circumstances between 1950 and 1978 China grew more quickly (6.9 percent per year) than the rest of the Global South. In addition it made remarkable social progress. In 1983 the World Bank (1983) declared that 'China's most remarkable achievement during the past three decades' was to have made 'low-income groups far better off in terms of basic needs than their counterparts in most other poor countries'. China was not totally egalitarian. China operated an eight-grade wage system. In addition there were many status, regional and rural-urban differences. Differences in income in cash and kind were however not large in accordance with the principle of common prosperity, shared development and, in difficult times, shared sacrifice.

Importantly in that era life expectancy increased from 35 in 1949 to 57 in 1957 and 68 in 1981, while China's population increased from 554.4 million to 1,014 million. According to the World Bank, 1979 life expectancy of 64 was higher than the average of 51 for low-income countries and 61 for middle-income countries. Adult literacy stood at 66 percent compared with 39 percent in low income and 72 percent in middle income countries. Net primary school enrolment (93 percent) was just short of that for industrialised countries (94 percent). In 1978 per capita rural income stood at ¥134 Yuan (PPS$81), while the per capita income of urban residents was ¥343.4 (PPS$208), yet the latter increased to ¥454.2 if one included the value of welfare, medical and other in-kind provision (Zhang, 1994).

At that stage however China remained a relatively poor country compared with the rest of the world. As in the case of other less developed countries, a major aim of the CPC and the Chinese government was to close the gap between China and relatively more developed countries. China had started to open up with the improvement in relationships with the United States in the early 1970s. Then at the very end of 1978, it formally decided to embark on a path of reform and opening up to accelerate the four modernisations (of agriculture, industry, science and technology, and defence) and increase the speed at which China caught up with the most prosperous countries. In this light it was argued in an article in the People's

Daily entitled 'A Few Getting Rich First and Common Prosperity' (一部分先富裕和共同富裕) that some people and some places should be allowed to get rich first, with the others getting rich later.

At that time however Deng repeated his oft-made statement (while also seeing through a new 1982 constitution confirming the centrality of a people-oriented democratic dictatorship). In a reflection on the decision to allow some people and places to get rich first, he said:

> In short, predominance of public ownership and common prosperity are the two fundamental socialist principles that we must adhere to. The aim of socialism is to make all our people prosperous, not to create polarization. If our policies led to polarization, it would mean that we had failed; if a new bourgeoisie emerged, it would mean that we had strayed from the right path. In encouraging some regions to become prosperous first, we intend that they should inspire others to follow their example and that all of them should help economically backward regions to develop. The same holds good for some individuals (Deng, 2014 [1985]).

China's new course delivered historically unprecedented economic growth. China grew on average at 9.9 percent per year from 1978 to 2008. By 2023 it was an upper middle-income country with a Gross Domestic Product (GDP) per head at Purchasing Power Parity (PPP) of US$19,082 (29 per cent of the United States figure of $66,762). At present it is expected to join the ranks of high-income economies during the country's 14th Five-Year Plan (2021-25) period. And at PPP it is already the largest economy in the world.

In the years from 1978 to the present as a whole, the path the CPC chose saw overall increases in the real incomes of virtually all Chinese people, although not in all periods (as in the 1990s the real incomes of some groups declined as did access of rural people to public services). Incomes increased however at very different speeds - although in China one should never forget the very considerable importance of the universal property rights of rural households and until the 1990s of employees' workplace (danwei) rights that provide/provided significant in-kind income.

In China as in other parts of the world, marketisation, liberalisation and the development of the private economy were accompanied by increases in inequality. A difference with other parts of the world was however that in China, due to the management by the CPC and the Chinese government of its integration into the world economy, an outcome was significant national economic growth.

Allowing some people and places to get rich first did however see the gaps between cities and the countryside increase strongly as did gaps between regions (due to the concentration of growth in large cities in coastal areas). China's Gini coefficient also increased strongly (Figures 1 and 2 below). In the 1990s and in the new millennium the number and scale of mass incidents (relating to employment, land acquisition, demolitions,

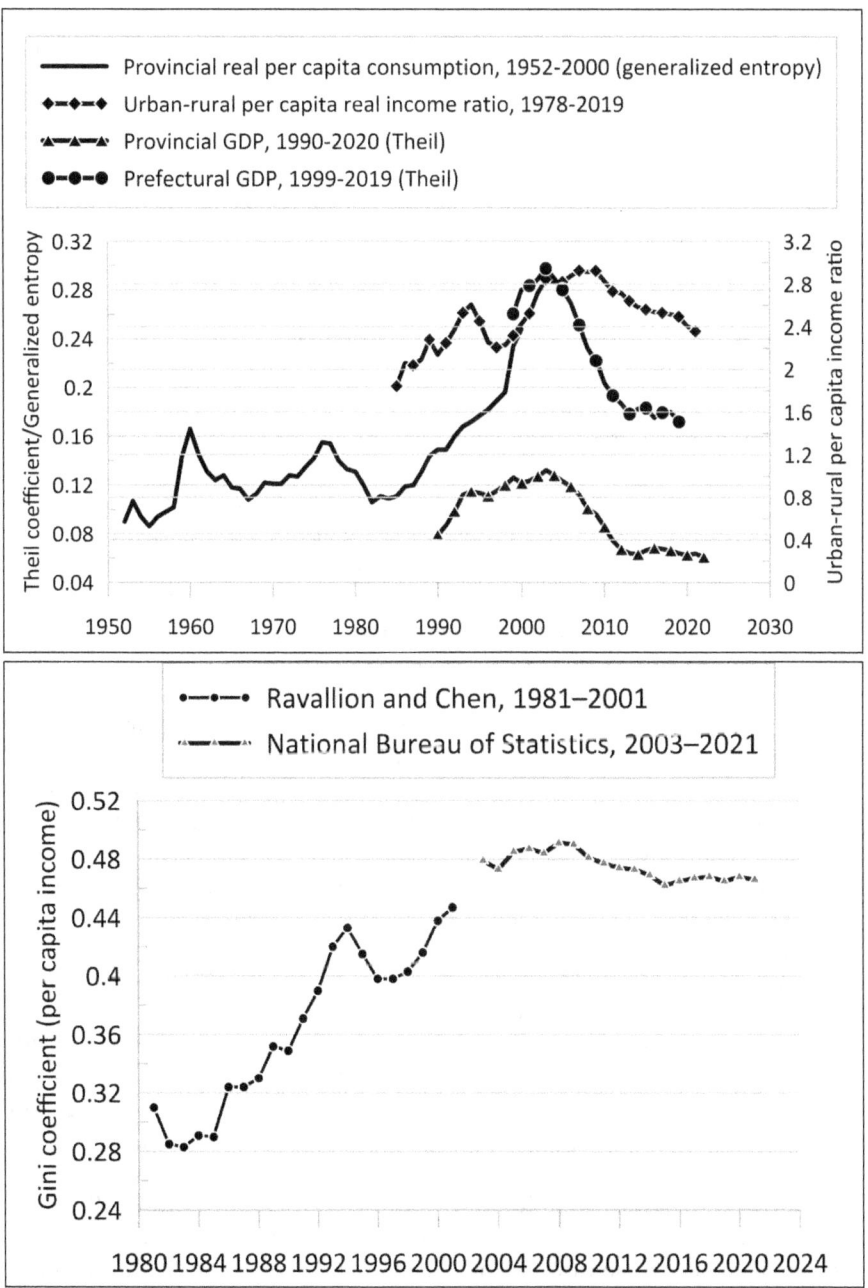

environmental pollution and official misconduct) also increased. In many cases the expansion of capital was not sufficiently regulated. In this context it is important to recall that markets are incapable of distinguishing between useful and spurious uses of resources: all that matters is that the purchaser wants something and can pay for it. Moreover competing claims are settled solely in terms of ability to pay, while the ability to pay depends on the distribution of income.

In this situation government guidance is vital. As Mao Zedong (Mao, 1975) said in speaking of the development of a commodity economy: 'Such things can only be restricted under the dictatorship of the proletariat' which means under a political party and a strong government that are people-centric rather than capital-centric. In this statement one can see the extraordinary importance of the incorporation of the Four Cardinal Principles into China's new constitution, ensuring not just that reform and opening up was managed so as to achieve positive overall economic outcomes but also that China's development would be channelled along a path that would serve all of its people.[1]

In 1999, in the aftermath of the Asian Financial crisis, the CPC started to pay much greater attention to urban-rural and regional disparities in the name of common prosperity. To address the 'three rural problems' (三农问题), the government supported massive counter-cyclical public investment in rural infrastructure, reformed land rights, improved rural public services, implemented a policy to establish a new socialist countryside, and introduced a New Rural Co-operative Medical System and minimum life guarantees. In 1999 development of the western region was set in motion to expand domestic demand, drive economic growth and contribute to common prosperity. In quick succession regional development programmes for Northeast and Central China were implemented.

The results were striking and indicative of the remarkable effectiveness of government policy. In 2004 interprovincial and inter-prefectural disparities started to fall, although the centres of older smokestack industries in the Northeast continued to decline. In 2007 urban-rural disparities started to diminish. The income Gini coefficient which had stood at less than 0.3 in the early 1980s continued to rise until 2008 when it reached 0.49, after which it stabilised or declined slowly. The income and wealth Gini coefficients, however, remained large (see Figures 1 and 2).

As for the composition of the rich, most are entrepreneurs whose wealth derived from private sector activity (reflecting therefore the distribution of economic assets) along with superstars in the world of media and entertainment. Corruption and monopolies also play a role but are not the root cause.

After the Eighteenth National Congress (2012) in a more challenging international environment (the United States had again labelled China as a strategic rival whose development it planned to contain) China entered a new era under the leadership of Xi Jinping. The emphasis on common prosperity increased strongly alongside recognition of the vital importance of high-quality development: 在高质量发展中促进共同富裕 [in a context of high-quality development promote common prosperity] in the words of Xi Jinping. Moreover, the CPC came to define common prosperity (and indeed China's modernisation path) not just in material but also in governance, ecological, cultural and spiritual terms, as China strives to move in the direction of a high-income country, a very high quality of life and the rejuvenation of Chinese civilisation.

In advice to Zhejiang Province on the establishment of a demonstration zone for common prosperity and high quality development, the State Council Information Office of the People's Republic of China (2021) mentioned eight issues and twenty-eight measures. The first aspect concerned the guiding ideology, adherence to overall party leadership and the goals of high-quality development, a high quality of life, ecological civilization and spiritual civilization rooted in socialist ideals and Chinese civilisation. As an experimental area for the reform of the income distribution system, the Opinions called for adherence to the principle that distribution depends mainly on work and protection of compensation of labour which coexists alongside other sources of income where improved policies are required, continuous increases in urban and rural incomes and a narrowing of the income gap. Also development goals were set for 2025 and 2035 by when Zhejiang is expected reach a GDP per capita equal to economically advanced countries.

The second point was that the quality and efficiency of development are to lay the material foundations for common prosperity. The Opinions called for vigorous improvements in independent innovation, scientific and technological self-reliance and self-improvement, the establishment with strategic support of new competitive advantages and the consolidation and expansion of the real economy, increased economic efficiency, and increased vitality of market actors giving 'full play to the strategic supporting role of the state-owned economy and preventing the 'disorderly expansion of capital'.

The third aspect was deepening reform of the income distribution system and increasing the income of rural and urban residents through multiple channels. The document specified fuller and higher quality employment, life-long education and training, collective wage bargaining and an increase in labour compensation, continuous improvements in incomes, expansion of middle-income groups, an improved distribution system and encouraging the return to society of wealth and income (tertiary distribution).

The fourth point concerned the narrowing of the development gap between urban and rural areas and realizing the sharing of high-quality public services. The measures identified include equalisation of the provision of basic social services, integrated development of urban and rural areas, improved living conditions in the city and countryside including new urbanisation, adhering to the position that houses are for living and not for speculation, development of affordable housing and rural revitalisation with an ecological rational, collectively owned and cooperative rural economy, a strong social security system and improved assistance of less advanced by more advanced areas including stronger east (coast) west (mountain) counterpart assistance.

The fifth concerned development of a 'cultural highland in the new era' and an enrichment of people's spiritual and cultural life. Involved are socialist ideology and core socialist values and support for traditional Chinese culture, revolutionary culture and advanced socialist culture (at the expense of materialistic and individualistic culture).

The sixth aspect involved the practical application of the idea that 'lucid waters and green mountains are as precious as mountains of silver and gold' and the creation of a beautiful and liveable living environment. Stronger land-use planning and controls, improved spatial organisation, ecological protection, protection of arable land, reduced carbon emissions, green finance and recycling and a circular economy are all involved.

The seventh aspect refers to the Fengqiao experience [枫桥经验 – *fēngqiáo jīngyàn*], considered a model of rural governance that involves 'relying on the masses to resolve contradictions locally'. The aim is to improve governance capacity and efficiency with digital reform and establish a grassroots governance system which integrates autonomy, the rule of law, the rule of virtue and the rule of intelligence and improves democratic consultation; more generally, the construction of a Zhejiang under the rule of law and a safe Zhejiang.

The eight aspect concerns a series of safeguards: upholding and strengthening the overall leadership of the CPC, strengthening a system involving central government guidance and overall planning, provincial responsibility and implementation by cities and counties, improving approval and supervision mechanisms and establishing an evaluation system.

In the next steps a plan was fleshed out by the provincial government, a leadership group and individual departments and local government. In July 2021, Zhejiang Province launched a road map aiming amongst other things to increase provincial residents' per capita disposable income to 75,000 yuan ($11,560) by 2025, raise the compensation of labour to more than 50 percent of GDP, increase higher education enrolment to more than 70 percent and reduce personal health expenditure below 26 percent of total expenditure. The first set of 28 pilot projects were announced, and municipal governments were asked to outline their three-year plans to make achievements that could be replicated and promoted in other cities.

Ahead of this step however, shortly after the start of the new era and the increased emphasis on common prosperity, a concern for those who had been left behind in China's modernisation was reflected in a major new poverty alleviation programme. China has implemented poverty alleviation programmes ever since the establishment of the new China. Over time the number of poor people has declined as these programmes helped lift people out of poverty, but the poverty count also rose as the poverty threshold was raised.

In 2013-14, China embarked on a new eight year (2013-20) targeted poverty alleviation (jīngzhǔn fúpín) programme to lift all of the 98.99 million people who lay below the 2010 poverty line above the line and to lift all of the 129,000 poverty-stricken villages and 832 impoverished counties out of poverty (M. Dunford, Gao, & Li, 2020). At that stage China already provided welfare assistance to people who for good reasons could not meet their essential needs. It also provides public services for all, and in the poverty campaign did a great deal to provide good quality housing for poverty-stricken households, sometimes in places that were more accessible to services and for those who could work employment opportunities. The campaign, which was underpinned by ambitious programmes of infrastructure provision and itself involved major commitments of financial resources and energy and work on the part of government cadres, was remarkable in that it achieved its objectives, often raising household incomes well over the poverty threshold. Moreover it did so in large part by enabling and assisting the development of economic activities and employment opportunities that permitted those who could work to lift themselves out of poverty. At that stage however the commitment did not end but is carried forward in programmes for rural regeneration.

In December 2020, at the Central Economic Work Conference, Xi Jinping tasked government agencies with curbing the 'disorderly expansion of capital'. Xi also emphasised other important economic tasks including strengthening technological innovation, increasing domestic demand and moving in the direction of carbon neutrality and ecological civilization.

To address the 'disorderly expansion of capital' in 2021 a series of important actions were carried out. These actions included major crackdowns. Measures were adopted to address the undesirable and monopolistic conduct of technology companies, the internet platform economy and other sectors (online food delivery, car and truck hailing, recruitment). Other measures were directed at the real estate sector (establishing red lines to control debt and associated risks) and financial capital (shadow banking). Yet other measures restricted the actions of owners seeking to get rich by going public on foreign stock markets and reduce excessive incomes. Housing and education were other targets where it was said that the latter had to some degree been 'hijacked' by capital.

These measures addressed serious problems. Housing, education and health costs amounted to three mountains whose costs had exploded as a result of liberalization and inadequate supervision and which were crowding other domestic household expenditure. The large increase in the cost of raising children was also a disincentive to couples giving birth to more than one child. Measures to control property development and management and private finance and speculation were designed not just to reduce the risks of real estate and financial markets crises but also to address the unaffordability of housing and the existence of unoccupied housing. In May 2021 the use of crypto currencies was banned, and in June 2021 crypto-mining operations were shuttered. In addition some large corporations were allowed to teeter towards default.

As already mentioned, common prosperity is seen as an integral part of a new high-quality and high productivity modernisation path where each part depends on the others. The Chinese government is aware that the world is on the verge of a new industrial revolution, at a time when the past drivers of Chinese growth (the low-wage export processing industries, real estate and the consumer platform economy) have lost momentum and had evolved in some respects in undesirable directions.

China's response is the development of qualitatively new high quality productive forces: new technologies and drivers of economic development associated with a fourth industrial revolution including the integration of digital and real technologies, new energy, quantum computing, electric vehicles, artificial intelligence, robotics, aerospace and life sciences among others.

To play a leading role in this new industrial revolution China is integrating industry, academia and research, increasing the role of innovation in research and development and industrial design, integrating as mentioned digital, real and green technologies, accelerating the transformation of scientific and technological achievements into real productive forces, improving scientific, technical and vocational education and providing patient long-term finance. In these tasks the state-owned economy is an institutional guarantee of rapid development of productive forces as China's investment share testifies (as well as helping limit social polarisation). At the same time this sector will co-exist alongside a variety of other types of property including foreign and private capital and widespread innovative entrepreneurship. In short the aims of the Chinese government are a profound supply-side structural transformation of the Chinese economy, new growth drivers and a new more equitable modernisation path.

Achieving high-quality development also entails 'ecological civilization': green and healthy ways of life and production and a harmonious coexistence of people and nature. Accordingly, the CPC is putting in place a very strict system of land and space management, promoting a human-centred National New Urbanization Plan (2014–2020) involving city and urban-rural integration, while the 19th National Congress called for a major rural revitalization strategy, recognizing the vital role of the countryside as a source of necessities of life, as a characteristic of Chinese civilization and as a place where large numbers of Chinese people will continue to work and enjoy happy lives.

New productive forces can radically increase productivity and therefore real income. As briefly mentioned however a great deal of attention is paid not just to increasing real income but also to the reshaping of the distribution of income. On this score the CPC aims to restrict unreasonably high incomes and has conducted an important anti-corruption campaign. This campaign included a three-year programme to 'Combat organised crime and root out local Mafia' [打击有组织犯罪，铲除当地黑手党] addressing rent-seeking relationships between government and business. The management of cultural and entertainment industries was strengthened and negative aspects of celebrity culture including tax evasion are being addressed along with steps to encourage young people to pay more attention to scientific, technical and cultural pursuits.

The Chinese government identifies three channels of income distribution: the primary, secondary and tertiary distribution. As a socialist country most emphasis is placed on the primary distribution and on the importance of the contribution of everyone capable of working to the collective work of Chinese society. Also important is that the wage share should comprise a large share of national income and serve as the main channel of income distribution. In this light the quest for common prosperity is often associated with measures designed to expand the number of middle-income households and move in the direction of an olive-shaped distribution of income - reducing the spread of incomes relative to the median. Other measures seek to prevent employers from imposing excessive hours of work. Although an increase in low incomes is mentioned, more attention should perhaps be paid to more secure and higher incomes for low income groups and in particular to enabling them to gain social esteem and respect for their contributions and to live decent, dignified and happy lives. Indeed in an era in which China's growth will depend more on the growth of the domestic market, increases in very low incomes would also contribute significantly to market expansion and China's future economic progress.

The primary distribution of income also includes other income streams: rents, interest profits and dividends. Of these considerable attention is paid to the mobilisation of collective resources especially in rural communities to develop income-generating activities whose earnings are shared by the entire village community, although clearly the scope for such initiatives is greater in rural areas close to larger cities or close to scenic places that attract large tourist flows.

The CPC and the Chinese government also shape the distribution of income by acting on the secondary distribution, comprising government taxation and expenditure. The CPC has established a social security system that includes subsistence allowances for those who due to age or incapacity cannot support themselves and 'five types of insurance and one fund' (五

险一金) (namely a pension and health employee and resident schemes), unemployment, work injury and maternity insurance as well as a housing provident fund that increased from covering 52.4 percent in 2014 to almost all today. On the supply side, public infrastructures and services (medical and health care, education, elderly care, emergency services, culture and sports, waste management, transport and so on) have been established across the length and breadth of China. At present standards vary but attempts are made to equalise them. The finance of these infrastructures and services does however give rise to important challenges concerning the system of taxation especially in the light of a decline in the revenues that local governments can raise from the rights to use state-owned land and the limited contribution of personal income taxation. Other issues under consideration include taxes on property and capital gains.

The CPC has for a long time emphasised the role of tertiary distribution stressing the responsibility of those who get well-off first to help those who were left behind to themselves become rich. These steps have yielded fruit in many ways and in many places. Highly successful examples are associated with China's counterpart assistance programmes under which rich cities and provinces are required to assist and support less prosperous areas. At the same time there are very significant inter-regional tax transfers made by the central government to local government in less prosperous parts of China.

Common prosperity and high-quality development are in short key elements of the path on which the Chinese government under the leadership of the CPC has embarked especially in the new era as it strives to move in the direction of a high-income country, a very high quality of life and the rejuvenation of Chinese civilization. These two broad goals are multi-dimensional.

The steps already adopted involve a conception of common prosperity that involves material, ecological, cultural, spiritual and governance progress. Improvements in the distribution of income involve rewarding contributions and hard work, while containing excessively high and especially illicit incomes. The rich will remain rich but the poor should no longer continue to be poor: the size of middle income groups should increase and low incomes should rise as part of a more domestically oriented model of development.

With the onset of the COVID-19 pandemic, the protection of human life and management of health risks added another dimension. At present a wide range of policy experiments are under way in Zhejiang Province which was established as a demonstration zone for common prosperity in 2021 (as detailed above), while moreover China's call for a shared community of human destiny (the resuscitation of shared histories, the exploration of a shared present, and the articulation of a shared future) are a counterpart of common prosperity in the international arena.

REFERENCES

Deng, X. (1999). *gòngtóng fùyù lǐlùn yánjiū [共同富裕理论研究 – Research on the Theory of Common Prosperity]*. Beijing: zhōnghuá gōngshāng liánhé chūbǎnshè [中华工商联合出版社 – China Federation of Industry and Commerce Press].

Deng, X. (2014 [1985]). Unity depends on ideals and discipline, 7th March, 1985. In X. Deng (Ed.), *Selected works of Deng Xiaoping* (Vol. III (1982-1992)). Beijing: People's Publishing House.

Dunford, M. (2022). The Chinese Path to Common Prosperity. *International Critical Thought*, 12(1), 35-54. doi:10.1080/21598282.2022.2025561

Dunford, M., Gao, B. Y., & Li, W. B. (2020). Who, where and why? Characterizing China's rural population and residual rural poverty. *Area Development and Policy*, 5(1), 89-118. doi:10.1080/23792949.2019.1571425

Mao, Z. (1975). *mǎkèsī, ēngésī, liènìng lùn wúchǎnjiējí zhuānzhèng* [马克思，恩格斯，列宁论无产阶级专政 – Marx, Engels and Lenin theory of the dictatorship of the proletariat. *hóng qí* [红旗 - Red Flag], 3, 2-19.

Marx, K. (1952 [1891, 1847]). *Wage labour and capital* (F. Engels, Trans.). Moscow: Progress Publishers.

Tang, M. D., Michael] (2023). 中国推进共同富裕 [*zhōngguó tuījìn gòngtóng fùyù* – China promotes common prosperity]. 马克思主义及其中国化理论研究 and 世界马克思主义研究 [*World Marxist Studies*], 2022, 82-91.

The State Council Information Office of the People's Republic of China. (2021). 中共中央国务院关于支持浙江高质量发展建设共同富裕示范区的意见 [*zhōnggòng zhōngyāng guówùyuàn guānyú zhīchí zhèjiāng gāo zhìliàng fāzhǎn jiànshè gòngtóng fùyù shìfànqū de yìjiàn* – Opinion of the State Council of the People's Republic of China on supporting high quality development and construction of a common prosperity demonstration zone in Zhejiang]. Retrieved from Beijing:

The World Bank. (1983). *China. Socialist economic development: The economy, statistical system, and basic data (English)*. Retrieved from Washington D.C.: https://documents1.worldbank.org/curated/en/192611468769173749/pdf/multi-page.pdf

Wèi, X. (2021). 只有公有制才能消除两极分化，实现共同富裕 (toutiao.com) [*zhǐ yǒu gōngyǒuzhì cái néng xiāochú liǎngjífēnhuà, shíxiàn gòngtóng fùyù -*

only public ownership can eliminate polarization and achieve common prosperity].

Zhang, X. (1994). *Analysis of urban-rural income disparities [chéng xiāng shōurù chājù fēnxī]*. Beijing: China National Bureau of Statistics [zhōng guó guó jiā tǒng jì jú].

NOTES

1. The Four Cardinal Principles are: keeping to the path of socialism; upholding the people's democratic dictatorship; upholding the leadership of the Communist Party of China; and upholding Marxism-Leninism and Mao Zedong Thought.

THIS PAGE INTENTIONALLY LEFT BLANK

8

Mao, China, and the development of Marxism-Leninism

By J. Sykes

It is a fundamental point of scientific socialism that revolutionary theory is essential to revolutionary practice. Practice is both the source and aim of Marxist-Leninist theory. The two are inextricably linked, and to break that link by privileging one at the expense of the other means disarming the revolutionary movement. Indeed, "Theory is the experience of the working-class movement in all countries taken in its general aspect."[1] Marxism is a science, based on the theoretical analysis and summation of material processes, of real practice in the real world, and its reason for existence is likewise to inform and serve the needs of the practical revolutionary movement for socialism.

By applying Marxism to the concrete problems of the Chinese revolution, Mao Zedong developed and enriched Marxist-Leninist theory in a number of important ways. The Communist Party of China refers to Mao's contributions, together with his comrades such as Zhou Enlai, Liu Shaoqi, Zhu De, Chen Yun, and Deng Xiaoping, as "Mao Zedong Thought", arguing that they represent the "sinicisation of Marxism." While that's true, Mao's contributions are also universal. The theory-practice dialectic in fact goes both ways. By applying Marxism-Leninism to the concrete conditions of China, Marxism-Leninism itself was also further developed and enriched.

Mao's contributions to revolutionary theory are not limited to the

Chinese context. They have been studied closely by revolutionaries all over the world, and applied by those revolutionaries to their own particular conditions. Indeed, many of Mao's most important contributions are universal in scope. Mao further developed our understanding of dialectical and historical materialism, our understanding of revolutionary socialist strategy, and the Marxist theory of the state and the transition to socialism. In what follows, we will break down and examine Mao's contributions to Marxism in each of these areas.

Dialectical Materialism

It is appropriate to begin with Mao's contributions to our understanding of dialectical materialism, the philosophical foundation of Marxism. Dialectical materialism is basically the methodology that Marxism relies upon to analyse social reality. To understand Mao's contribution we will need to have a clear understanding of what exactly dialectical materialism is and the role it plays in Marxist theory since Marx.

It is important to note that Marx did not invent dialectics, but rather Marx takes dialectics from the German idealist philosopher G.W.F. Hegel, who in turn borrowed and elaborated on ideas from Ancient Greece. He stripped the idealist framework of Hegel's philosophy away and placed dialectics on a materialist basis. However, Karl Marx wrote no treatise on dialectics. He never truly explained his dialectical materialist methodology. Rather, he simply put it to work in his own analysis. Reading through his works one sees it at work everywhere, from *The German Ideology* through the monumental *Capital*, but he never really explains or outlines its elements or how they function in any detail. This task would be left primarily to his collaborator, Friedrich Engels. It is mainly in two works that Engels explains dialectical materialism, namely the books *Anti-Duhring* and *Dialectics of Nature*.

Engels explained dialectical materialism first and foremost by breaking it down into its constituent parts: dialectics and materialism. It is materialist in that it is based on an examination of concrete, material processes. It is dialectical in that it sees those processes as interconnected and driven primarily by the struggle between opposing forces within them, forces that are in contradiction to one another.

Engels further explained dialectics in terms of three dialectical laws, and these three laws would form the basis of how dialectical materialism was discussed through the early 20th century. These laws are 1) "the law of the unity and interpenetration of opposites," 2) "the law of the transformation of quantity into quality," and 3) "the law of the negation of the negation."

While Mao Zedong wrote a number of works dealing with philosophical problems, his main philosophical works are *On Practice* and *On Contradiction*. These essays are distilled from lectures Mao gave to the Anti-Japanese Military and Political College in the Yenan base area during the United

Front against Japan. His purpose was to teach the cadres of the Communist Party of China how to apply Marxist theory to the complex reality of the Chinese revolution in a particularly dynamic and volatile period. This meant combating both dogmatism and empiricism in understanding the relationship between theory and practice.

While *On Practice* deals with Marxist epistemology, that is, the Marxist theory of knowledge, *On Contradiction* gives us a systematic and extremely practical explanation of dialectical materialism. In *On Contradiction* Mao explains dialectics in terms that we haven't seen before. He explains that reality is made of various interconnected processes driven by internal contradictions. However, he explains that complex processes contain many contradictions working at the same time, which he calls the principal and secondary contradictions. Principal contradictions are those that determine the overall motion of the process, while secondary contradictions are also at work, but these "occupy a secondary and subordinate position". The principal contradiction in capitalist society, Mao explains, is the contradiction between the bourgeoisie and the proletariat. Other contradictions also exist, but it is this class contradiction that determines the overall motion of capitalist society.

Mao further explains that any given contradiction is itself asymmetric. It is unbalanced and develops unevenly. Of the two aspects of the contradiction, one side will be dominant, the principal aspect of the contradiction, while the other, secondary aspect, will be subordinate to the principal aspect. For example, under capitalism, in the contradiction between the bourgeoisie and the proletariat, the bourgeoisie is dominant, and so is the principal aspect of the contradiction. It controls the state, its military and police, and the dominant ideology of society serves to reinforce its power.

However, Mao explains that the principal and secondary aspects of a contradiction can exchange places. In the course of socialist revolution, the bourgeoisie and the proletariat do just that. The proletariat, formerly the secondary aspect, dominated by the bourgeois class dictatorship, overthrows its former oppressor and itself becomes the dominant, principal aspect, exercising its own state power over the bourgeoisie in the process of socialist construction. It does that, Mao explains, in a "qualitative leap." By increasing its force, quantitatively, it is able to change the situation qualitatively, changing the very nature of society in the course of a socialist revolution. This is the way that Mao explains dialectical change, through the transformation of quantity into quality whereby the principal and secondary aspects of a contradiction exchange places.

It is noteworthy that this explanation of dialectics leaves out the third law given to us by Engels, the "law of the negation of the negation". While it is a controversial point, it is this author's view that by presenting a materialist dialectic freed from the reliance on the "negation of the negation" Mao in fact completes the project begun by Marx, by which dialectics is placed on a materialist basis, freed from its Hegelian "mystic shell". Indeed, in his "Talks on Questions of Philosophy" Mao makes this explicit.

> Engels talked about the three categories, but as for me I don't believe in two of those categories. (The unity of opposites is the most basic law, the transformation of quality and quantity into one another is the unity of the opposites quality and quantity, and the negation of the negation does not exist at all.) ... The most basic thing is the unity of opposites. The transformation of quality and quantity into one another is the unity of the opposites quality and quantity. There is no such thing as the negation of the negation. Affirmation, negation, affirmation, negation ... in the development of things, every link in the chain of events is both affirmation and negation.

Elsewhere I've explained Mao's meaning here in depth,[2] and there is not space to go too deeply into it here. The main thing to stress is that, for Mao, social change is explained by the transformation of quantity into quality, which is a function of contradiction, since it is the moment in which the principal and secondary aspect of a contradiction exchange places. Second, Mao breaks from a linear and metaphysical framework that still clings to dialectical materialism as long as it relies upon the negation of the negation to explain change. Instead, Mao presents us with a fundamentally non-linear dialectic, in presenting us with an understanding of society as a complex matrix of contradictory forces, teeming with myriad and unevenly developed contradictions. In *On Contradiction*, Mao strips Marxism-Leninism of any last vestiges of Hegelianism and grounds its methodology on a scientific basis.

Historical Materialism and Ideology

Historical materialism, or the materialist conception of history, is the application of the dialectical materialist methodology to understanding history and its laws of motion. Prior to Marx, people accounted for historical change as the product of shifts in people's ideas. Marx, however, understood that in fact the changes in our ideas were the product of changes in our material reality. The dominant ideology of any given society reflected the thinking of the dominant class in that particular historical mode of production, and that ideology then served to reinforce the domination of that class and its hold on the mode of production. Based on the methodological framework he developed in *On Contradiction*, Mao was able to clearly articulate the way in which ideology also developed unevenly in class society. He puts this succinctly when he says that, "in class society, everyone lives as a member of a particular class, and every kind of thinking, without exception, is stamped with the brand of a class."[3] In other words, bourgeois and proletarian ideology both exist in contradiction to one another. They both arise from the class struggle, and each serve their own class interests. However, because the bourgeoisie is dominant in capitalist society, its ideology, liberalism, is also dominant. And yet, the proletarian ideology, Marxism, exists alongside it in a subordinate position. Because bourgeois ideology is dominant, it exerts tremendous pressure on the thinking of working and oppressed people under capitalism, putting its own limits on what is deemed possible. Indeed, wherever both classes exist, both ideologies will exist and be in conflict. This is true under capitalism, where bourgeois ideology is dominant, and it is true as well under socialism, where proletarian ideology becomes dominant.

Revolutionary Strategy

Regarding revolutionary strategy, Mao made contributions in at least three important areas that we will address here. First, he developed the theory of the mass line, which connects the Marxist theory of knowledge to organisation, strategy and tactics. Second, he further developed the theory of the United Front, which he understood as one of the most important weapons of the revolutionary movement. Third, he made important contributions to revolutionary military strategy in the course of the Chinese Revolution, which are broadly applicable to other semi-feudal and semi-colonial countries like China was. In his essay "Introducing the Communist" Mao wrote that "our eighteen years of experience have taught us that the united front, armed struggle and Party building are the Chinese Communist Party's three 'magic weapons'"[4] and it is in this framework that we should understand these three contributions.

The mass line relates fundamentally to solving the challenges of party building in the course of the revolution. The Marxist-Leninist party is a disciplined, revolutionary party organised according to democratic centralism, and it is guided by revolutionary theory, criticism and self-criticism, and the mass line. It is through the mass line that the party connects with the masses, both learning from the masses and leading the masses. Mao explains the mass line most clearly in his essay "Some Questions Concerning Methods of Leadership", where he writes:

> In all the practical work of our Party, all correct leadership
> is necessarily "from the masses, to the masses". This means:
> take the ideas of the masses (scattered and unsystematic
> ideas) and concentrate them (through study turn them into
> concentrated and systematic ideas), then go to the masses and
> propagate and explain these ideas until the masses embrace
> them as their own, hold fast to them and translate them into
> action, and test the correctness of these ideas in such action.
> Then once again concentrate ideas from the masses and once

again go to the masses so that the ideas are persevered in and carried through. And so on, over and over again in an endless spiral, with the ideas becoming more correct, more vital and richer each time. Such is the Marxist theory of knowledge."[5]

Mao further explains how this can be carried out. "The masses in any given place are generally composed of three parts, the relatively active, the intermediate and the relatively backward," writes Mao. "The leaders must therefore be skilled in uniting the small number of active elements around the leadership and must rely on them to raise the level of the intermediate element and to win over the backward elements."[6] From this, Mao derives a very important point: "A leading group that is genuinely united and linked with the masses can be formed only gradually in the process of mass struggle, and not in isolation from it." While this method of leadership isn't new to Marxism, and in fact has been practiced by all successful revolutionaries since the Bolshevik Revolution, Mao was the first to so clearly and systematically explain it in this way.

In other words, revolutionaries should use Marxist theory to analyse the balance of forces and locate the key struggles, then unite with felt needs and immediate demands of the advanced, active elements among the toiling and oppressed masses within those struggles. They can then rely upon these advanced fighters among the masses to draw in the broader intermediate element, and win over or isolate the backwards. Thus party building is inextricably linked with mass struggle. Here the demands of the masses are engaged directly. The masses are organised and mobilised to confront the class enemy. The lessons of these struggles are brought home to the masses, and through this process the consciousness and organisation of the masses is elevated. Furthermore, it is through this process that the advanced are won over to Marxism-Leninism, bringing the leaders of the working class into the revolutionary movement, and thereby building the party.

This party stands at the centre of a broad united front. This is a united front of different class forces, and Mao explains this best in his essay *Analysis of Classes in Chinese Society* where he works to determine which classes are friends and which classes are enemies of the working class in China.[7] Concretely, in terms of contemporary Western capitalist societies, this united front is often made up of mass organisations such as trade unions, anti-war groups, groups organising for community control of the police and against police crimes, and so on. These mass organisations in the united front have much broader unity than what is possible for the party itself, and so they allow the party, through persuasion and example, to lead a much broader section of the masses than the party itself could be due to its very high standards of unity and discipline. But Mao is particularly clear that the other forces in the united front also represent other class interests, such as those of the petite bourgeoisie or, in the case of oppressed nations, the national bourgeoisie. While these other class forces can be drawn into a united front against a common enemy (imperialism, or monopoly capitalism), it is essential for the party to maintain "independence and initiative."[8] In other words, leadership of the united front cannot be handed over to other class forces. Only the party of the working class can accomplish the historic task of overthrowing capitalism and advancing through socialism to a society without exploitation, classes, and class struggle. It is not in the material interest of any other class to carry out such a programme – although it should be noted that, in the case of semi-colonial semi-feudal pre-revolutionary China, the material interest of the bulk of the peasantry was served by adopting proletarian ideology and allying with the working class in the overthrow of feudalism and the construction of socialism.

Finally, Mao is clear on the necessity of revolutionary armed struggle, and develops the theory of protracted war, explaining how a small and weak force can grow to become a strong force by developing the armed struggle through the stages of strategic defence, strategic equilibrium, and strategic offensive. This is mainly developed in *On Protracted War* and *Problems of Strategy in China's Revolutionary War*. This theory of protracted people's war is applicable broadly to large, semi-colonial and semi-feudal countries with a large peasantry, who are fighting for national liberation and socialism.

Problems of Socialist Construction

Immediately after the defeat of the Kuomintang government and the foundation of the People's Republic of China in 1949, the Communist Party of China was faced with some unique challenges. First, the material conditions of the country were such that it was a majority peasant country with underdeveloped productive forces. Its basic class structure prior to the victory of the revolution was semi-colonial and semi-feudal. As a result, Mao understood that socialist construction had to be preceded by a period of what he called "New Democracy" with the aim of eliminating the vestiges of feudalism and colonialism. New Democracy meant developing a government led by the working class in alliance with the peasantry, the petite bourgeoisie, and the national bourgeoisie. This established a "system of people's congresses, from the national people's congress down to the provincial, county, district and township people's congresses, with all levels electing their respective governmental bodies".[9]

Mao also emphasised that socialism itself develops through stages. "It is possible to divide the transition from capitalism to communism into two stages: one from capitalism to socialism, which could be called underdeveloped socialism; and one from socialism to communism, that is, from comparatively underdeveloped socialism to comparatively developed socialism, namely, communism." Mao goes on to explain that "this latter stage may take even longer than the first. But once it has been passed through, material production and spiritual prosperity will be most ample. People's communist consciousness will be greatly raised, and they will be ready to enter the highest stage of communism."[10] Developing from this, Xi Jinping further emphasises this point in saying, "while applying the basic tenets of Marxism to the practical problems of China, our Party came to realise that the development of socialism is a continuous historical process made up of different stages."[11] This understanding of developing socialism through successive stages continues to inform China's planning and development as they work to develop the productive forces and eliminate scarcity.

Following both Lenin and Stalin, Mao also emphasised that class struggle continues under socialism, primarily in the superstructure. In *On the Correct Handling of Contradictions Among the People*, Mao outlined how different types of contradictions, antagonistic contradictions between the people and the enemy, and non-antagonistic contradictions among the people themselves, ought to be handled. He emphasised that non-antagonistic contradictions should be handled by democratic and persuasive methods, emphasising the struggle for unity.

Ultra-left errors were made during the period of the Cultural Revolution, spanning the decade from 1966 to 1976, but lessons can be learned from this period. One of the most important lessons to learn is that the revolutionisation of the superstructure, including cultural revolution, ought to be a gradual process under the guidance of the party, and that stability and development must be safeguarded. The Cultural Revolution further facilitated a backlash, culminating in the disturbances at Tiananmen Square in 1989, where right opportunists led by Zhao Ziyang attempted to restore capitalism. Deng Xiaoping led the CPC in defeating counterrevolution and emphasised the "four cardinal principles": upholding the socialist road, upholding the people's democratic dictatorship, upholding the leadership of the Communist Party, and upholding Marxism-Leninism Mao Zedong Thought. These principles still guide the People's Republic of China today.

The defense of Marxism-Leninism against Modern Revisionism

After the death of Stalin in 1953, the Soviet Union began a long process of ideological degeneration beginning with the rise of Khrushchev and the 20th Congress of Communist Party of the Soviet Union in 1956 and culminating in the liquidation of the USSR under Gorbachev and Yeltsin in 1991 with the complete restoration of capitalism. From the late 1950s onward, Mao Zedong led the international communist movement in the defence of Marxism-Leninism.

Some significant mistakes were made by the Communist Party of China in this period. Most importantly, the CPC prematurely concluded that capitalism had been restored in the Soviet Union, eventually going so far as to calling the Soviet Union "social imperialist" and "social fascist." The great U.S. Marxist-Leninist theorist Harry Haywood provided a very succinct refutation of this error, when he wrote in 1984 that "without a monopoly capitalist class and without capitalist relations of production there is no fundamental and compelling logic in the Soviet economy that creates a need to export capital and exploit other countries through trade. As a result it also has no colonies and no empire to sustain."[12]

In spite of this error, the polemics that the Communist Party of China contributed to the "Great Debate" from 1956 to 1964 are important contributions to the defence of Marxism-Leninism against revisionist distortions. These articles, written with Mao's guidance, showed exactly what was at stake in Khrushchev's "party of the whole people" and "state of the whole people", which denied the nature of the CPSU and USSR as a proletarian party and proletarian dictatorship. Further, these polemics also challenged Khrushchev in his opportunist formulation/interpretation of "peaceful competition", "peaceful coexistence", and "peaceful transition from capitalism to socialism", and explained how these theories departed from Marxism-Leninism and represented capitulation to and collaboration with imperialism.

During this period revolutionaries all over the world took inspiration from Mao Zedong's leadership, taking his "little red book", *Quotations from Chairman Mao Zedong,* as a handbook for leading revolutionary struggle.

Conclusion

Mao Zedong's contributions to Marxism-Leninism were developed in the crucible of the Chinese revolution, but are not limited only to the Chinese context. While "Mao Zedong Thought" continues to guide the Communist Party of China, Mao's contributions to Marxism-Leninism are also essential to helping guide revolutionaries all over the world. While some erroneously argue that Mao's contribution represent a new stage in the development of Marxism, like Leninism did before, it is true that many of Mao's contributions to Marxism-Leninism are universally applicable and represent the further development and enrichment of Marxism-Leninism as a whole. Though we are still in the era of imperialism and proletarian revolution, the era of Marxism-Leninism, Mao should be given his place as one of Marxism's essential theorists. Indeed, every revolutionary can benefit from studying Mao's writings and by examining how the theory he helped develop can be creatively applied to their own concrete conditions.

NOTES

1. J.V. Stalin, "The Foundations of Leninism." *Works*, volume 6. Foreign Languages Publishing House. Moscow, 1953. p.92
2. J. Sykes, *The Revolutionary Science of Marxism-Leninism*. FRSO. Minneapolis, 2023. p 54.
3. Mao Zedong, "On Practice." *Selected Works of Mao Zedong*, volume 1. Foreign Languages Press. Beijing, 1967. p. 296.
4. Mao Zedong, "Introducing *The Communist*." *Selected Works of Mao Zedong*, volume 2. Foreign Languages Press. Beijing, 1965. p. 288.
5. Mao Zedong, "Some Questions Concerning Methods of Leadership." *Selected Works of Mao Zedong*, volume 3. Foreign Languages Press. Beijing, 1967. p. 119.
6. Ibid, p. 118.
7. Mao Zedong, "Analysis of Classes in Chinese Society." *Selected Works of Mao Zedong*, volume 1. Foreign Languages Press. Beijing, 1967. p. 13.
8. Mao Zedong, "The Question of Independence and Initiative Within the United Front." *Selected Works of Mao Zedong*, volume 2. Foreign Languages Press. Beijing, 1965. p. 213.
9. Mao, "On New Democracy." *Selected Works of Mao Zedong*, volume 2. Foreign Languages Press. Beijing, 1965. p. 352.
10. Mao, "Reading Notes on the Soviet Textbook *Political Economy*." *Selected Works of Mao Zedong*, volume 8, Foreign Languages Press. Paris, 2020. p.339.
11. Xi Jinping, "On the New Development Stage Philosophy and Dynamic" *Selected Readings from the Works of Xi Jinping*. Foreign Languages Press. Beijing, 2024. p.433.
12. Harry Haywood, "China and Its Supporters Were Wrong About USSR" *The Guardian* (New York) April 11, 1984.

9

Building socialism, building the ecological civilisation
China's revolutionary path to sustainable development

Efe Can Gürcan

Introduction

GLOBAL CAPITALISM IS CURRENTLY GRAPPLING with an unprecedented convergence of crises. These challenges range from the lingering economic repercussions of the Great Recession and the COVID-19 pandemic to the mounting geopolitical tensions between great powers. Equally consequential is the pressing problem of mass displacement affecting countless individuals, which only compounds the complexity of these challenges. Meanwhile, one of the most visible and pressing dimensions of these converging crises is the grave ecological consequences resulting from climate change and the pervasive issue of food insecurity afflicting hundreds of millions of people worldwide.

The period 2011-2020 is designated as the warmest decade ever recorded (World Meteorological Organisation, 2023). In 2023, the world experienced its hottest year on record by a significant margin, with records shattered for ocean heat, sea level rise, Antarctic sea ice loss, and glacier retreat, leading to unprecedented extreme weather events impacting every part of the globe (World Meteorological Organisation, 2024; World Weather Attribution, 2023). In 2022, food inflation soared to its highest level high since 1990 (Reuters, 2023), and despite some recovery, May 2024 levels remain comparable to those during the global food crises of 2007-2008 and 2010-2012 (Trading Economics, 2024b). In 2023, nearly 282 million people across 59 countries and territories suffered from acute hunger, a rise of 24 million from the previous year. Extreme weather events were the primary cause of food insecurity affecting 18 countries and over 77 million people, compared to 57 million in 12 countries in 2022 (FOA, 2024).

In our contemporary world, unrestrained capitalism and free-market anarchy have undoubtedly emerged as the primary catalysts for a multitude of converging crises that imperil the very survival of humanity, including the global climate and food crises. The relentless pursuit of profit maximisation, inherent in our current economic system, has proven inadequate in addressing these profound challenges. Therefore, it is beyond doubt that the pressing issues of environmental degradation, socio-economic inequality, and global instability demand solutions that extend beyond the myopic scope of profit-driven motives.

In this precarious setting, socialism has never been as pertinent as it is today. For one thing, a robust state apparatus is essential to navigate and resolve these crises effectively. Only through the strategic and efficient guidance of public policies can we hope to steer society as well as the private sector toward sustainable and equitable practices. The state's role in regulating and directing economic activity is indispensable in fostering a harmonious balance between development and sustainability. In this context, socialist China has emerged as an exemplary model of economic development inspiring much of the developing world. Since 1979, China is the only major country that has remained untouched by any economic crisis, thanks to its socialist system. The 1979-2018 period witnessed to an average economic growth rate of 9.4 percent, making China the world's second-largest economy, top producer, and the leading exporter of technological goods (Gürcan, 2021).

Development can be broadly understood as a process of positive socio-economic change aimed at improving the standards of life, which begins with addressing our most basic necessities, such as food, water, shelter, and healthcare. It is therefore inherently a socialist concept. Moreover, the environment plays a crucial role in achieving and maintaining high standards of life encapsulated in the notions of development and socialism. In simplest terms, access to a clean and healthy environment is fundamental to human well-being. Without it, the basic necessities of life are compromised, and the socio-economic progress required for development becomes unattainable. A polluted or degraded environment directly impacts health, reduces economic opportunities, and exacerbates social inequalities (Dale, 2002). Within this framework, sustainable development can be understood as "the integration of environmental health, social equity and economic vitality in order to create thriving, healthy, diverse and resilient communities for this generation and generations to come" (UCLA Sustainability, 2024). This concept extends beyond traditional notions of human development by incorporating an environment-centred approach, requiring an eco-socialist perspective on the well-being of society that is intrinsically linked to the health of our natural surroundings.

Against this backdrop, the Chinese model of socialism presents a compelling example of how meaningful and systematic state intervention can lead to significant advancements in sustainable development. China's approach offers valuable lessons for the rest of the world. It demonstrates how publicly driven governance policies can drive innovation, reduce poverty, and promote environmental sustainability under the leadership of a disciplined political party representing the working masses. Within this framework, the present chapter explores China's broader policy paradigm and its implementation in various areas.

China's 'Global Civilisation Initiative' and 'Ecological Civilisation'

Chinese socialism has already proposed concrete and comprehensive solutions to the global environmental crisis. The Global Civilisation Initiative (GCI), introduced by General Secretary Xi Jinping in his keynote address "Join Hands on the Path Towards Modernisation" at the CPC in Dialogue with World Political Parties High-Level Meeting on March 15, 2023, aims to advance human civilisations through responsibility, inclusiveness and mutual learning, responding to the urgent call of peoples around the globe for stronger solidarity and collaboration in facing common challenges, including ecological challenges (Liu, 2023). The GCI's core tenets are encapsulated in the "four advocatings": advocating respect for the diversity of civilisations, advocating the common values of humanity, advocating the importance of the inheritance and innovation of civilisations, and advocating robust international people-to-people exchanges and cooperation (Liu, 2023).

Importantly, China's framework of ecological civilisation (生态文明, *shengtai wenming*), which should be seen as an integral part of the Global Civilisation Initiative, underscores the critical link between human civilisation and ecological conditions. In the face of the global environmental crisis, an ecological vision grounded in the four advocatings becomes indispensable. This vision includes advocating respect for biodiversity and the environment, reasserting our shared ecological values, emphasising the importance of environmental inheritance and innovation, and promoting robust international cooperation to achieve sustainable development.

The term "ecological civilisation" was coined by Iring Fetscher, a German Marxist political scientist, who defined it as "the dialectics of progress and reflection on industrial civilisation" (Y. Li et al., 2023)a bibliometric map of related articles published between 2000 and 2019 was mapped according to the identities of the collected Chinese and international bibliographies (9196 in CNKI and 664 in WoS. It later resurfaced in the Soviet Union in the early 1980s and was adopted by Chinese agricultural economist Qianji Ye in 1987 and officially used by the State Environmental Protection Administration (SEPA). At the 15th National Congress in 1997, the Communist Party of China (CPC) identified "sustainable development" as a crucial strategy for China's modernisation efforts. The concept of ecological civilisation began to take shape among Chinese scholars in the 1990s and gained political traction in 2003 when Pan Yue, then director of SEPA, introduced the idea of eco-industrial civilisation. In China, the concept gained further traction under the administration of Hu Jintao (2003-2013), who in his report to the 17th National Congress of the CPC introduced the idea of a "harmonious society", drawing from traditional Chinese philosophy of harmony between humans and nature (天人合一思想). Hu's vision of a harmonious society extended beyond social equality and justice to include balanced development across urban and rural areas, regions, socio-economic spheres, human-nature relations, and domestic and international contexts (Gürcan, 2021; Han & Sheng, 2023; Yang et al., 2017). This notion resonated with Mao Zedong's (1956) principles of balanced development as articulated in his speech "On the Ten Great Relationships", where he argues that success in building socialism depends on policy makers' ability to adequately address all the prevailing disequilibria and contradictions, such as the relationship between heavy industry on the one hand and light industry and agriculture on the other. In today's world, the contradiction between economic development and the environment is a significant issue, and it is crucial not to underestimate either side or neglect their importance.

Hu also proposed a "Scientific Outlook on Development", advocating a sustainable development model that prioritises people and the environment, leveraging science, technology, and education. He emphasised energy conservation and sustainable development as crucial for improving the quality of life in China. His "five-in-one" strategy integrated economic, political, cultural, and social construction with ecological civilisation, highlighting the interdependence of these elements for achieving long-term economic growth and social welfare (Gürcan, 2021).

Xi Jinping further strengthened Hu's emphasis on ecological civilisation, framing it as a cornerstone of the Chinese Dream and making it a priority task for the CPC in 2012. In the same year, the 18th National Congress officially declared the construction of ecological civilisation as a national strategy. This was later incorporated into the national environmental law in 2013. Xi's administration established the "Task Force for the Promotion of Economic Development and Ecological Civilisation" and in 2015, the CPC Politburo adopted the "Central Opinion Document on Ecological Civilisation Construction." This led to significant enforcement actions, including fines, detentions, and disciplinary measures against numerous companies and officials. Moreover, the 19th National Congress of the CPC in 2017 set goals for greening and beautifying China, based on principles of green development and ecological civilisation. During the Xi era, moreover, environmental issues became a strategic element of China's national security, reflected in the new "Holistic National Security Outlook" announced in 2013, which identified ecological security as one of eleven key areas. In a similar vein, China's "Made in China 2025" strategy, announced in 2015, aligns with Xi's holistic view of national security, focusing on green manufacturing and innovation across various strategic sectors, as well as his notion of "high-quality development," which indicates a historical transition from rapid growth to a period of greater efficiency, equity, sustainability and security. All of this includes not only socio-ecological progress but also new information technology, robotics, aerospace, marine engineering, railway equipment, energy-efficient vehicles, power equipment, new materials, biomedicine, medical devices, and agricultural machinery, aiming to integrate information technology with industry and promote internationalisation of manufacturing (Gürcan, 2021; Sheng & Cheng, 2024; Y. Zhang & Fu, 2023).

Since 2007, when the Ministry of Environmental Protection published the first policy document based on an ecological civilisation index system, China has continuously refined its ecological indicators. The 2013 introduction of specific indicators for demonstration zones marked a significant development. The system has evolved since 2019, featuring more targeted and assessable indicators, emphasising proportion of coastal waters with excellent water quality, coastal ecological restoration, resource conservation and utilisation, industrial recycling development, social progress, public satisfaction, a number of targeted policy plans, and civilised village style. These evolving indicators reflect China's growing emphasis on ecological civilisation in national policy, transitioning from a focus on economic development to integrating environmental governance and ecological security. This shift is evident in newly introduced categories such as "ecological space", which has driven reforms in territorial spatial planning (Bing, 2023).

In 2013, China embarked on a new path toward ecological construction with the establishment of Ecological Civilisation Pilot Zones. By 2014, Fujian, Jiangxi, Guizhou, Yunnan, and Qinghai were designated as provincial-level pilot zones. These national pilot zones represent an institutional strategy aimed at enhancing ecological and environmental protection across provinces, autonomous regions, and cities. This initiative seeks to address the challenges posed by administrative divisions in ecological governance. By improving air and water quality and other environmental factors, China aims to develop a model for building an ecological civilisation that is tailored to its unique national conditions. Research in these pilot zones reveals significant reductions in carbon dioxide emissions and energy consumption per unit of GDP, as well as increases in green areas and biodiversity (Gao et al., 2024; S. Li et al., 2023; Wang et al., 2023; P. Zhang et al., 2023; Y. Zhang & Fu, 2023).

Revolutionary Outcomes of Ecological Civilisation as a Policy Framework

In line with the Global Civilisation Initiative, China's key achievements on the path towards ecological civilisation involve a series of three unfolding and mutually conditioning revolutionary processes that also lead the way in international environmental cooperation. They include a clean energy revolution, a sustainable agricultural revolution, and a green urban revolution.

China's clean energy revolution, initiated with the 2005 Sustainable Energy Law and the 12th and 13th Five-Year Plans (2011-2020), has been noteworthy. By 2009, China became the leading global investor in sustainable energy technology, and in 2013, it was the top investor in clean energy with investments totalling $61.3 billion. By 2015, China had become the world's largest producer of solar, wind, and hydroelectric power (Gürcan, 2021). Thanks to Chinese supply, solar panel prices in 2024 have become significantly more affordable, costing half as much compared to the previous year (Nikkei Asia, 2024). In 2023, China installed more solar panels than the entire cumulative total in the United States. As a result of China's efforts, the costs of photovoltaic and wind power have dropped by more than 80 percent and 60 percent, respectively (EcoWatch, 2024).

Renewable energy capacity refers to the maximum generating capacity of installations that use renewable sources to generate electricity. According to 2023 data, China is by far the leading country in installed renewable energy capacity worldwide, with a capacity of 1,453 gigawatts as compared with the US capacity of 388 gigawatts as the second leading country (Statista, 2024d). Even though China's oil and coal consumption has peaked by 2023 as the world's largest coal consumer (nearly 55 percent of global consumption) and second largest oil consumer (CEIC Data, 2024; Statista, 2024a, 2024e), China leads the world in renewable energy consumption (including geothermal, wind, solar, biomass, and waste), with 13.3 exajoules in comparison with the US consumption of 8.43 exajoules in 2022. China is by far the leading consumer of hydropower, with over three times the consumption of other leading countries such as Canada and Brazil. Several of the world's hydroelectric dams with the highest generating capacity are located in China, many of which were constructed in the past two decades. The Three Gorges Dam on the Yangtze River was completed in 2012, becoming the largest in the world (Statista, 2024c). Accordingly, the share of China's primary energy consumption from renewable sources has grown precipitously, increasing from 5.3 percent in 2003 to 16.16 percent in 2023 (Our World in Data, 2024c). Moreover, China has drastically reduced its energy intensity (understood as primary energy consumption per unit of gross domestic product (GDP), in kilowatt-hours per dollar), from 2.44 kWh in 2005 to 1.65 kWh in 2022 (Our World in Data, 2024b). This performance points to more efficient energy use as a key indicator of improved energy efficiency and reduced environmental impact. Eventually, this has resulted in a significant reduction of carbon intensity of energy production measured in kilograms of CO_2 per kilowatt-hour, from 0.31 in 2003 to 26 in 2022 (Our World in Data, 2024a), while the growth rate of China's peaking CO_2 emissions (metric tons per capita) in 2020 has visibly slowed down since 2011 (World Bank, 2024a). One should also note that China ranks 38th among the world's biggest per capita carbon emitters, with a significantly lower performance (8 tonnes of CO_2) than the United States (14.9 tonnes of CO_2) and Canada (14.3 tonnes of CO_2) as leadings emitters (Visual Capitalist, 2023).

China is currently intensifying its focus on green agriculture to combat agricultural pollution and other environmental pressures. From 2005 to 2018, the area dedicated to organic agriculture in China increased by over 36 percent, from 2,301,300 to 3,135,000 hectares. This achievement surpasses that of other BRICS countries and the United States in this area (Gürcan, 2021). Among the countries on the Development Assistance Committee (DAC) list, furthermore, China has the third-largest area of organic agricultural land, covering 2.9 million hectares, following India with 4.73 million hectares and Argentina with 4.06 million hectares. China's success in organic farming is also evident as it boasts the third-largest organic market globally, valued at 12.4 billion euros, following the US at 58.6 billion euros and Germany at 15.3 billion euros. Similarly, China is home to 52 affiliates of International Federation of Organic Agriculture Movements (IFOAM) – Organics International, making it the second-largest number globally after Germany with 80 affiliates, and ahead of India with 49 affiliates and the US with 45 affiliates. China's success is also underscored by its leading role in organic aquaculture, with a production volume of 140,091 metric tons in 2022, making it the largest producer globally and contributing significantly to Asia's 43 percent share of total aquaculture production (FAO, 2024).

China's agricultural green revolution has been propelled by coordinated efforts from both central and local governments to make green agriculture a key part of their development strategies. This emphasis has also spurred the growth of the eco-village movement since the late 1980s, with China establishing 1,200 "pilot eco-villages" by 1990 and increasing that number to 2,000 by 2011. These initiatives were strengthened by policies promoting green labelling standards, including green food (*lüse shipin*), pollution-free food (*wugonghai shipin*), and organic food (*youji shipin*) during the 1990s. The Ministry of Agriculture introduced a green food programme in 1990 and founded the China Green Food Development Centre in 1992 to offer technical support and quality control (Gürcan, 2021).

By 2011, China had established 42 certification offices, 38 quality control terminals, and 71 environmental monitoring centres. The green food programme received additional support from the Risk-Free Food Action Plan in 2001, which aimed to reduce chemical pollution, improve food security, and speed up organic certification. The National Sustainable Agriculture Development Plan (2015-2030) provided a detailed blueprint for these initiatives. In 2017, the No. 1 Central Document, an annual policy paper issued by the Central Committee of the CPC and the State Council, elevated green and sustainable development to the second major development goal (Gürcan, 2021).

It is important to note that China's greening efforts are not limited to organic farming. China has shown a consistent and significant increase in its forested areas, with the proportion of total land area covered by forests rising from 16.7 percent in 1990 to 23.6 percent in 2021 (World Bank, 2024b). A similar trend can be seen in the expansion of parkland, which increased from less than 100,000 hectares to 673,000 hectares by 2022 (Statista, 2024b). By 2015, China had achieved the highest net increase in forest coverage of any country. China's forestry projects are thereby unmatched globally in their scale and ambition. These initiatives stand alone in their scope and reflect China's broader environmental strategy within the ecological civilisation framework. As such, China has been the leading contributor to global greening within its borders over the past two decades. These large-scale forestry projects exemplify China's unique environmental aspirations, deeply intertwined with national pride (Weins et al., 2023). Furthermore, it would be pertinent to add that China's protected areas currently cover 18 percent of its terrestrial territory (Green List, 2024), while the proportion of marine protected areas increased from 1.28 percent of the total surface area in 2008 to 5.5 percent in 2022 (Trading Economics, 2024a).

Importantly, China's progress in greening the nation is closely linked to its sustainable urbanisation strategy. Many Chinese cities have dropped down or out of the list of the most polluted cities, leaving India and Pakistan at the top. Among the world's most polluted cities, there are only two Chinese cities, namely Hotan (ranked 13th) and Kashgar (ranked 42nd) (IQAir, 2023). China's cities have also joined the ranks of those with the strongest sewage treatment capacity in the world. In addition, China has the most electric vehicles, bikes, and efficient public transportation. It is considered to be not only the world's centre of electric bus production and consumption but also as having cities with the world's longest subway systems (Gürcan, 2021). China also possesses the world's largest network system of high-speed railways (CNN, 2022). According to the 2023 Leadership in Energy and Environmental Design (LEED) rating system prepared by the US Green Building Council, China is the world's second leader in sustainable architecture (GBCI, 2024). Furthermore, the eco-city movement, initiated in 2003 by the Ministry of Environmental Protection, aims to create a low-carbon, circular economy by expanding green spaces, encouraging recycling, promoting sustainable architecture, and enhancing social welfare in urban areas. In 2009, only six of the world's 79 eco-cities were in China, but by 2011, this number had risen to 25. By 2015, China had developed or planned 284 of the world's 658 major eco-cities, accounting for over 43 percent of the total (Gürcan, 2021).

This movement has also strengthened China's multilateral environmental cooperation. Key projects include the Tianjin China-Singapore Eco-City, the Sino-Dutch Shenzhen Low-Carbon City, and the Sino-French Wuhan Ecological Demonstration City. These initiatives, particularly the development of eco-industrial parks, showcase environmental collaboration among developing countries and between developed and developing countries. The China-Singapore Suzhou Industrial Park incorporates green spaces and lakes, while the Sino-Singapore Tianjin Eco-City features systems for energy efficiency, green transportation, sustainable architecture, sewage treatment, and recycling (Gürcan, 2021).

China has established itself as a leader in multilateral environmental cooperation, particularly with the Association of Southeast Asian Nations (ASEAN). In 2009, China and ASEAN signed the Strategy on Environmental Cooperation, leading to the creation of the China-ASEAN Environmental Cooperation Centre. This was followed by the China-ASEAN Environmental Cooperation Action Plans for 2011-2013 and 2014-2015, and the 2016-2020 Strategy on Environmental Cooperation. These initiatives aimed to enhance regional collaboration in research, development, and eco-city construction. Additionally, the Green Silk Road Envoys Program was launched to promote staff training, scientific exchange, and political dialogue on sustainability, green innovation, entrepreneurship, biodiversity, and ecological protection (Gürcan, 2021).

Recently, China has intensified its multilateral environmental efforts through the Belt and Road Initiative (BRI). The 2015 "One Belt, One Road" document committed the BRI to greater environmental protection, biodiversity preservation, and climate change mitigation. Xi Jinping's 2016 call for a "green, healthy, intelligent, and peaceful" Silk Road led to the "Guidance on Promoting Green Belt and Road" and the implementation of the Green Action Plan and Maritime Cooperation Vision, focusing on maritime protection. As a result, the Second BRI Forum in 2019 established green investment principles (Gürcan, 2021).

The BRI respects the sovereignty of its participants by not imposing policies on them, instead encouraging voluntary adoption of the BRI's ecological civilisation principles. At the Second BRI Forum, members were invited to join initiatives like the International Green Development Coalition, the Sustainable Cities Alliance, the South-South Cooperation Initiative on Climate Change, the Environmental Technology Exchange and Transfer Centre, the Environmental Big Data Platform, and the Green Investment Fund. These initiatives gained momentum amid criticism that many BRI investments were directed toward carbon-intensive sectors and large-scale infrastructure projects that harmed local environments (Gürcan, 2021).

Green finance is a critical component of the BRI, encompassing bonds for sustainable projects, credits for sustainable investments, and insurance schemes for environmental disaster protection. China's green investment supports initiatives like low-carbon transportation, high-speed trains, clean energy projects, anti-pollution efforts, and clean coal investments. By 2019, China had become the global leader in green bonds and credits, surpassing the US (Gürcan, 2021).

The Asian Infrastructure Investment Bank (AIIB), Asia's first bank independent of Western control and the world's fourth-largest multilateral development bank, plays a crucial role in BRI financing. Established in 2016 under China's initiative, the AIIB aims to bridge the gap between supply and demand for Asian infrastructure spending, estimated at $8 trillion by 2020. The AIIB has embraced ecological civilisation by adopting the Environmental and Social Framework (ESF) in 2016 to encourage social and environmental sustainability, including a green economy, gender equality, and labour rights. The ESF emphasises balanced development, reducing fossil fuel use, environmental resilience, energy conservation, and biodiversity. At its second annual meeting in South Korea in 2016, the AIIB adopted the Sustainable Energy for Asia Strategy and approved its first loan to reduce coal use in China. The AIIB's fourth meeting in Luxembourg in 2019 reaffirmed its commitment to supporting the green economy. The AIIB's green funds include the $75 million Tata Cleantech Sustainable Infrastructure On-Lending Facility (India), $75 million Asia Investment Fund (Asia-wide), $100 million L&T Green Infrastructure On-Lending Facility (India), $200 million TSKB Sustainable Energy and Infrastructure On-Lending Facility (Türkiye), and $150 million India Infrastructure Fund (India). Additionally, the AIIB launched a $500 million AIIB Asia ESG Enhanced Credit Managed Portfolio (Asia-wide) and the $500 million Asia Climate Bond Portfolio to accelerate climate action and develop the climate bond market (Gürcan, 2021).

The AIIB's green framework also extends to sustainable urbanisation, green transportation, and rural sustainability. Examples include loans for India's Gujarat Rural Roads Project ($329 million), Metro Line Project ($335 million), Madhya Pradesh Rural Connectivity Project ($140 million), Andhra Pradesh Urban Water Supply and Septage Management Improvement Project ($400 million) and Andhra Pradesh Rural Roads Project ($445 million); Laos' National Road 13 Improvement and Maintenance Project ($40 million); Indonesia's National Slum Upgrading Project ($216.5 million); the Philippines' Metro Manila Flood Management Project ($270.6 million); Sri Lanka's Colombo Urban Regeneration Project ($200 million); and Bangladesh's Municipal Water Supply and Sanitation Project ($100 million) (Gürcan, 2021).

While the long-term impact of the AIIB and BRI on ecological civilisation is still uncertain, there is well-founded optimism given China's leadership in multilateral environmental cooperation. The AIIB's sustainability strategy is already being implemented through green funds across Asia. Since 2016, China's green investments as part of the BRI have increased, including solar panel projects in Vietnam, the Quaid e-Azam Solar Park and Jhimpir Wind Farm in Pakistan, the Aisha Wind Farm and Wolayita Sodo Power Transmission Line in Ethiopia, and similar projects in Thailand and Malaysia (Gürcan, 2021).

Conclusion

Despite possessing the second-largest economy in the world, China remains a developing country, and its journey toward sustainable development is far from perfect. This being said, the evidence suggests that China has made remarkable strides in sustainable development, even amid significant geopolitical challenges such as the US tech and trade wars, and geographical limitations including having only 7 percent of the world's arable land, 7 percent of the world's freshwater resources, and 8 percent of the world's natural resources that are essential for economic and ecological sustainability, such as minerals, metals and forests. Furthermore, only 19 percent of China's surface area is suitable for human habitation, with 65 percent being rugged terrain (Gürcan, 2021). Despite these challenges, China has emerged as a global leader in sustainable development, achieving historically significant tangible results that serve as a strong example for the developing world. These accomplishments would not have been possible under a free-market capitalist economy but have been realised through socialism.

China's strategy is rooted in an alternative vision of "ecological civilisation", which holds an immense potential to counteract "ecological imperialism". Ecological imperialism refers to the exploitation of labour and natural resources in the developing world by Western metropoles, which externalise the costs of production and resource extraction, leading to significant human and ecological suffering. This exploitation has been a hallmark of capitalism, with neoliberalism exacerbating these issues since the 1970s. Nonetheless, China has refused to be victimised by such policies. Through strong state guidance, China has been pursuing the "Chinese dream" of socialist welfare.

Western metropoles now engage in an ecological-imperialist campaign, blaming environmental degradation on developing countries, particularly China. This Western-centric narrative often undermines China's leading environmental efforts, which are pivotal in global welfare and combating poverty. Yet, the undeniable truth remains: China has recognised its environmental challenges and incorporated the concept of "ecological civilisation" into its national security strategy. This policy framework has driven China's exemplary success in initiating an ecological revolution standing on three pillars: a clean energy revolution, a sustainable agricultural revolution, and a green urban revolution, which are complemented with multilateral cooperation and governance efforts.

REFERENCES

Bing, X. (2023). Understanding ecological civilization in China: From political context to science. *Ambio, 52*(1), 1895–1909.

CEIC Data. (2024). *China Oil Consumption*. https://www.ceicdata.com/en/indicator/china/oil-consumption

CNN. (2022). *Past, present and future: The evolution of China's incredible high-speed rail network*. https://edition.cnn.com/travel/article/china-high-speed-rail-cmd/index.html

Dale, A. (2002). *At the Edge: Sustainable Development in the 21st Century*. University of British Columbia Press. https://doi.org/10.59962/9780774850025-004

EcoWatch. (2024). *China Installed More Solar Panels Last Year Than the US Has in Total*. https://www.ecowatch.com/china-new-solar-capacity-2023.html

FAO. (2024). *The World of Organic Agriculture 2024: Statistics and Emerging Trends*. Research Institute of Organic Agriculture FiBL and IFOAM – Organics International.

FAO. (2024). *Global Report on Food Crises: Acute hunger remains persistently high in 59 countries with 1 in 5 people assessed in need of critical urgent action.* https://www.fao.org/newsroom/detail/global-report-on-food-crises--acute-hunger-remains-persistently-high-in-59-countries-with-1-in-5-people-assessed-in-need-of-critical-urgent-action/en

Gao, Q., Zhang, R.-P., & Gao, L.-H. (2024). Can environmental policies improve marine ecological efficiency? Examining China's Ecological Civilization Pilot Zones. *Marine Pollution Bulletin, 203*, 116479. https://doi.org/10.1016/j.marpolbul.2024.116479

GBCI. (2024). *China Ranks First in the World for LEED Green Building in 2023*. https://www.gbci.org/china-ranks-first-world-leed-green-building-2023

Green List. (2024). *China*. https://iucngreenlist.org/country/china/#:~:text=China%20has%20a%20long%20history,18%25%20of%20China%27s%20terrestrial%20territory.

Gürcan, E. C. (2021). On the Development of China's Environmental Policies Towards an Ecological Civilization. *Belt & Road Initiative Quarterly, 2*(3), 7–25.

Han, X., & Sheng, J. (2023). Governing the Future through 'Ecological civilization': Anticipatory Politics and China's Great Yangtze River Protection Programme. *Journal of Contemporary China*, 1–16. https://doi.org/10.1080/10670564.2023.2232747

IQAir. (2023). *World's most polluted cities*. https://www.iqair.com/world-most-polluted-cities

Li, S., Wang, D., & Wu, Q. (2023). Effect of ecological civilization pilot demonstration area construction on urban land green use efficiency. *Frontiers in Environmental Science*, *11*, 1200171. https://doi.org/10.3389/fenvs.2023.1200171

Li, Y., Tang, Y.-T., Tan-Mullins, M., & Ives, C. D. (2023). Exploring the Potential Opportunities of China's Environmental Agenda, Ecological Civilization, on Global Sustainable Development. *Sustainability*, *15*(6), 5135. https://doi.org/10.3390/su15065135

Liu, J. (2023). *Work Actively to Implement the Global Civilization Initiative and Jointly Advance Human Civilizations*. China Daily. https://global.chinadaily.com.cn/a/202304/13/WS64373f5ba31057c47ebb9ce5.html

Mao, Z. (1956). *On the ten major relationships*. https://www.marxists.org/reference/archive/mao/selected-works/volume-5/mswv5_51.htm

Nikkei Asia. (2024). *China solar panel glut squeezes European suppliers as prices plunge*. https://asia.nikkei.com/Business/Energy/China-solar-panel-glut-squeezes-European-suppliers-as-prices-plunge

Our World in Data. (2024a). *China: Carbon intensity: How much carbon does it emit per unit of energy?* https://ourworldindata.org/energy/country/china#carbon-intensity-how-much-carbon-does-it-emit-per-unit-of-energy

Our World in Data. (2024b). *China: Energy intensity: How much energy does it use per unit of GDP?* https://ourworldindata.org/energy/country/china#energy-intensity-how-much-energy-does-it-use-per-unit-of-gdp

Our World in Data. (2024c). *China: How much of the country's energy comes from renewables?* https://ourworldindata.org/energy/country/china#how-much-of-the-country-s-energy-comes-from-renewables

Reuters. (2023). *World food prices hit record high in 2022*. https://www.reuters.com/markets/world-food-prices-hit-record-high-2022-despite-december-fall-2023-01-06/

Sheng, J., & Cheng, Q. (2024). National Parks as the materialized imaginary of ecological civilization in China. *Environmental Science & Policy, 152*, 103660. https://doi.org/10.1016/j.envsci.2023.103660

Statista. (2024a). *Consumption of coal in China from 1998 to 2023 (in exajoules)*. https://www.statista.com/statistics/265491/chinese-coal-consumption-in-oil-equivalent/

Statista. (2024b). *Land area taken up by parks in China from 1990 to 2022 (in hectares)*. https://www.statista.com/statistics/225525/land-area-taken-up-by-parks-in-china/

Statista. (2024c). *Leading countries by renewable energy consumption worldwide in 2022 (in exajoules)*. https://www.statista.com/statistics/237090/renewable-energy-consumption-of-the-top-15-countries/

Statista. (2024d). *Leading countries in installed renewable energy capacity worldwide in 2023 (in gigawatts)*. https://www.statista.com/statistics/267233/renewable-energy-capacity-worldwide-by-country/#:~:text=The%20leading%20countries%20for%20installed,capacity%20of%20around%20388%20gigawatts.

Statista. (2024e). *Leading oil-consuming countries worldwide in 2022 (in 1,000 barrels per day)*. https://www.statista.com/statistics/271622/countries-with-the-highest-oil-consumption-in-2012/

Trading Economics. (2024a). *China—Marine Protected Areas (% Of Total Surface Area)*. https://tradingeconomics.com/china/marine-protected-areas-percent-of-total-surface-area-wb-data.html

Trading Economics. (2024b). *World Food Price Index*. https://tradingeconomics.com/world/food-price-index#:~:text=Food%20Price%20Index%20in%20World%20averaged%2087.37%20Index%20Points%20from,for%20World%20Food%20Price%20Index.

UCLA Sustainability. (2024). *What is Sustainability?* https://www.sustain.ucla.edu/what-is-sustainability/

Visual Capitalist. (2023). *Ranked: Per Capita Carbon Emissions by Country*. https://www.visualcapitalist.com/ranked-per-capita-carbon-emissions-by-country/

Wang, X., Yang, S., Yang, R., & Yang, Z. (2023). Analysis of the Spatiotemporal Evolution and Factors Influencing Ecological Land in

Northwest Yunnan from the Perspective of Leading the Construction of a National Ecological Civilization. *Diversity*, *15*(10), 1074. https://doi.org/10.3390/d15101074

Weins, N. W., Zhu, A. L., Qian, J., Barbi Seleguim, F., & Da Costa Ferreira, L. (2023). Ecological Civilization in the making: The 'construction' of China's climate-forestry nexus. *Environmental Sociology*, *9*(1), 6–19. https://doi.org/10.1080/23251042.2022.2124623

World Bank. (2024a). *CO2 emissions (metric tons per capita)—China, United States*. https://data.worldbank.org/indicator/EN.ATM.CO2E.PC?locations=CN-US

World Bank. (2024b). *Forest area (% of land area)—China*. https://data.worldbank.org/indicator/AG.LND.FRST.ZS?locations=CN

World Meteorological Organization. (2023). *The Global Climate 2011-2020: A decade of accelerating climate change*. WMO.

World Meteorological Organization. (2024). *Climate change indicators reached record levels in 2023: WMO*. https://wmo.int/news/media-centre/climate-change-indicators-reached-record-levels-2023-wmo

World Weather Attribution. (2023). *Climate change fuelled extreme weather in 2023; expect more records in 2024*. https://www.worldweatherattribution.org/climate-change-fuelled-extreme-weather-in-2023-expect-more-records-in-2024/

Yang, B., Xu, T., & Shi, L. (2017). Analysis on sustainable urban development levels and trends in China's cities. *Journal of Cleaner Production*, *141*, 868–880. https://doi.org/10.1016/j.jclepro.2016.09.121

Zhang, P., Tan, L., & Liu, F. (2023). Assessing the Implications of Ecological Civilization Pilots in Urban Green Energy Industry on Carbon Emission Mitigation: Evidence from China. *Energies*, *16*(22), 7638. https://doi.org/10.3390/en16227638

Zhang, Y., & Fu, B. (2023). Impact of China's establishment of ecological civilization pilot zones on carbon dioxide emissions. *Journal of Environmental Management*, *325*, 116652. https://doi.org/10.1016/j.jenvman.2022.116652

10

Patient finance: Beijing's core challenge to the Washington Consensus

Radhika Desai

The domestic and international operation of China's financial system is arguably the weightiest part of its challenge to the neoliberal Washington Consensus. However, this is not widely appreciated. Enumerations of the principal elements of the Washington Consensus list privatisation, cuts in social spending, deregulation, trade liberalisation, tight monetary and fiscal policies, rollback of labour and environmental regulation and the like. And while Chinese policy does form a contrast, and challenge, to these, by far the more important contrast and challenge is to the Western, predominantly US dollar denominated, international financial system. In any economic system, bank-industry relations are a critical determinant of the quality and quantity of investment, and that, in turn, largely determines the pace and pattern, the quantity and quality, of growth. So, the character of the financial system could not be more important.

Historically, there have been two distinct, indeed opposite, types of financial systems that have been contrasted by many, including Marx (1894/1981) and Hilferding (1910/1981 see also Desai and Hudson 2021). The first, inherited by capitalist societies from the pre-capitalist past, as Marx observed, is short term, predatory and speculative. It persisted into the capitalist era because its inability to provide more than short term commercial credit did not pose an obstacle to the early development of capitalism when individual fortunes sufficed for investment. Marx had anticipated that capitalism would soon outgrow this system and devise one suitable for its own productive expansion, and Hilferding was able to describe and analyse it in the early twentieth century when it emerged, classically in Germany. He called this new system 'finance capital' and contrasted this 'continental' system with the 'British' short-termist financial system which still prevailed in that country.

Finance capital was more suited to advanced capitalism involving very large investments for the long-term. It has characterised all the vigorously expanding productive systems of modern times, including, famously, Germany and Japan in their eras of fast growth. It provides long-term, 'patient' capital for productive industrial investment. Historically, moreover, both the main national currencies that have tried (without lasting success) to pose as world money – the pound sterling and the US dollar – have been based on the short-termist type of financial system. Only its short-term structures and practices are capable of the quick gyrations of policy that are necessary to permit a national currency to pose as a world currency, at least for a short time (in the case of the pound sterling, this was so even though it had the privilege of vast colonial surpluses that eased its operation). Financial systems of the 'finance capital' type, providing long-term patient capital, have historically not even attempted to play this role as their money is far less liquid, tied up as it is in long-term productive investment. They have internationalised the use of their currencies only to a limited extent to serve their productive economies in their international dealings.

As an instance of the first or short-termist type of system, the international financial system based in the US and operating in US dollars has been the post-1971 foundation for the US dollar's world role. The dollar's post-war link to gold, having become defunct by the late 1950s thanks to the US's balance of payments deficits which devalued the dollar and led creditors to demand gold, precisely as Robert Triffin, the Belgian economist who first identified this problem, argued, had to be formally broken in 1971, after exhausting a whole series of expedients to save it. Since then, the dollar's world role has relied on an enormous, not to say monstrous, expansion of the US dollar denominated financial system so as to draw money into it and support the dollar's value. In doing so, however, it set back productive economies everywhere and set back development in the developing world particularly. After all, unproductive financial activity preys upon incomes and revenues from production without expanding it; indeed, it even hinders productive expansion in so far as it diverts money from productive to financial investment.

In addition to being the arbiter of productive expansion and development, the US dollar denominated financial system is a more practical and persistent enforcer of the Washington Consensus – through the operation of bond markets or the political activities of investors – than any of the powerful agencies – whether the governments of the world's leading capitalist countries, or the EU or the IMF or the World Bank – which can entice or compel other governments to adopt it. China's financial system, by contrast, has not only powered its own spectacular development, financing productive expansion, technological innovation and even environmental protection but, through China's lending abroad in recent decades, has been offering the developing world a developmental alternative to anti-developmental Western finance.

Inevitably, as China's own economic success and its international lending have grown, Western and US discourses have sought to distort understanding of China's financial system in both its domestic and international operations. An initial phase of ambiguity, if not enthusiasm, about China lasted as long as the West and the US could believe that enfolding China into their embrace would make it neoliberal and capitalist. This phase climaxed in talk of 'Chimerica', referring to the alleged trade and financial inter-dependence of the Chinese and US economies (Ferguson and Schularick 2007). After the North Atlantic Financial Crisis of 2008, and certainly after Obama's 2012 'Pivot to Asia', however, there was a distinct change in tone.

Not only did the economic relationship prove less symbiotic and more one-sided as the US remained mired in stagnation after 2008 while China resumed robust growth after a sharp but short trade shock. It also became clear that China had its own ideas about its development path and, while it involved employing many market mechanisms, considerable private economic activity and even very large privately-run corporations, full-fledged neoliberalism was not among them. The Chinese state continued to plan and control the economy from its commanding heights, kept private activity oriented towards its goals and managed international trade and capital flows. Moreover, unlike the Soviet leadership (see Kotz and Weir 1997), the Chinese did not throw in the towel and instead strained to avoid that fate (Tsang 2016). As this realisation sank in and the economic contrast between US debility and Chinese dynamism sharpened, President Obama announced his 'Pivot to Asia', Western commentary on China turned hostile, President Trump declared a New Cold War against China and President Biden turned out to be an even more devoted prosecutor of it. Today, not only are sections of the US and Western capitalist classes threatened by China's increasing technological prowess, the need to distract large swaths of the working class electorate hurt by the West's own neoliberal policies of the past four decades has made China-baiting a regular feature of Western and US political discourses. These are the parameters that shape Western and US discourses about China in general and its financial system in particular.

Three major misunderstandings are generated about the Chinese financial system in the West. First, it is claimed that China supports the very dollar-denominated system that is based on the opposite type of financial arrangements by pointing to its sizeable dollar reserves. Secondly, China's financial system is portrayed as antiquated and inefficient. Finally, the undoubted overexpansion of China's real estate sector in recent years is seen as setting the stage for a 2008 style financial and real estate crisis, followed by a growth slump of the sort that continues to afflict Western economies today.

In what follows, we first outline how the dollar denominated financial system has worked in recent times and how it systematically sets back development in the developing world. Then, we will show how fundamentally different China's financial system is and close with debunking the myths about it that are in wide circulation today.

The Dollar-denominated international financial system and the developing world

The workings of the dollar system after 1971 required a vast expansion of predatory and speculative financial activity, and the developing world was, from the start, among its chief victims. In the 1970s, financial activity expanded by lending to the Third World on an unprecedented scale. This was not because it needed the capital, which it indeed did. However, the needs of the Third World are never uppermost in the minds of decision makers in Western financial institutions. They lent to earn interest on the vast oil revenues that were deposited with them after oil prices were jacked up in response to the swooning dollar. Entirely inadvertently, therefore, for a brief time, the Third World benefitted from practically free money thanks to the negative real interest rates that prevailed in the 1970s (making Western financial institutions even more desperate for a positive return on their hoards of otherwise unemployable capital). And many countries did indeed use this capital for industrial investment.

However, this inadvertently beneficial phase came to an abrupt end when, at the end of the decade, Federal Reserve Chairman Paul Volcker allowed interest rates to spike sharply by restricting money supply to stall the dollar's inflation-induced decline. This spike, which sent interest rates from negative territory to acutely positive levels (they touched 20 percent at one point), triggered the Third World Debt Crisis of 1982, formally inaugurated by the default of Brazil, Mexico and Argentina.

This crisis was resolved in a remarkably one-sided manner. Whereas credit relationships involve responsibility on both the debtor and creditor sides, the powers and activities of the IMF and the World Bank were expanded to make them bailiffs for the Western financial institutions, absolving the latter of responsibility for the crisis and imposing repayment schedules and new loans on the debtor governments on harsher terms that meant that often these countries repaid many times more than they borrowed. Thanks to development-retarding Structural Adjustment Programmes, which these institutions also imposed on the debtor countries, they had to do so while their development was set back, imposing cruel declines in material welfare on their inhabitants. The 1980s and, for many countries, even the 1990s, were veritable 'lost decades' of development and acute human misery.

After this episode, financial activity began expanding in new ways. Since direct bank lending had exposed Western financial institutions to bad debts on a scale that could easily have led to their collapse had it not been for the roles of their governments and the IMF and World Bank, they now resorted to securitised lending in dollar denominated bond markets. Western financial institutions have also sought to enter the financial markets of developing and 'emerging' economies so as to siphon off their incomes. And, as if these forms of extraction were not enough, they have also inflated various asset bubbles in the US itself – the dot com bubble of the 1990s, the housing and credit bubbles of the 2000s and the 'everything bubble' since – so rich people and financial institutions around the world can bring their money to the veritable (rigged) casino that is the US dollar denominated financial system.

To work, this system requires the free movement of capital into and out of as many countries as possible. Once capital flows are liberalised, Western financial institutions enter these countries and exert further pressure on host governments to deregulate the financial sector and so expand their ability to extract rentier and speculative gains from these economies.

The liberalisation of capital flows is usually justified as permitting much-needed investment capital to flow in. However, as the 'Big Emerging Markets' like South Korea, Indonesia and Thailand, which the Clinton administration targeted in its drive to have capital controls lifted, found out amid the East Asian Financial Crisis of 1997-8, the reality is quite the opposite. Though capital flowed in after they lifted capital controls, and though it was encouraged by the IMF, World Bank and many other financial institutions praising the excellent 'fundamentals' of these economies, most of it flowed not towards productive investment that might also bring in new technology, skills etc. but into these countries' asset markets. There it inflated the prices of existing assets, whether financial or real estate, creating huge bubbles as the skyrocketing prices of these assets lost any relation to their values.

As critical and cautious observers (like Rohatyn 1994) pointed out at the time, most investors knew little about these new markets. Inevitably, they were as easily spooked as they were enticed. When they took fright on some quite incidental and minor economic bad news, they stampeded out of these economies just as they had stampeded in. Capital inflows had already caused these countries' currencies to appreciate, affecting all-important exports adversely. The stampede out led, however, to currency and financial crashes that triggered deep economic crises lasting a decade or more.

All this economic damage was caused by capital flows that bypassed the productive economy almost entirely. And it was not all. In the aftermath of these crises, rather than roll back the changes that had led to them, beginning with re-imposing capital controls (as Malaysia did), these countries kept capital accounts open, seeking only to protect themselves from the possibility of future currency and financial crises by accumulating reserves. They would be used to buy the country's currency when others were selling, thus supporting its value. However, not only did this involve putting money in low-yielding dollar denominated 'liquid' assets that could be mobilised at short notice when foreign investors indulged in a major sell-off, it involved withholding precious capital from productive investment to maintain their connection with the dollar-denominated financial system.

In the twenty-first century, the system has developed new tentacles. With the Federal Reserve pursuing low or zero interest rate policies (LIRP or ZIRP) because the 'wealth effects' of successive bubbles they help inflate have been the only drivers of what growth there is in the US economy, many countries have been encouraged to borrow on international bond markets in dollars. As before, the real purpose of these loans is not to expand developing countries' fiscal options or improve their corporations' access to capital. Rather, it is to provide international investors with opportunities for higher returns in a low interest rate environment without having to commit to long-term productive investment. Not only are developing country borrowers generally considered 'risky' and so have to pay higher interest rates, the economic policies of the borrowing governments are now exposed to the whims of bond markets which like to keep them on the neoliberal straight and narrow. Finally, as countries like Sri Lanka are finding out at their cost, with the Federal Reserve raising interest rates in recent years, money flees these 'risky' markets, inducing a new round of debt crises.

Does China support the Dollar System?

It should be clear by now that over the past five decades or so, the dollar denominated financial system, all Western protestation to the contrary notwithstanding, serves not to direct capital into the developing world but rather acts as a giant vacuum cleaner, sucking up capital from the rest of the world and pouring it into the US dollar denominated financial system. This is done not only, as widely discussed, to cover the US's twin (balance of payments and fiscal) deficits with capital account inflows, but even more importantly, to keep markets for US dollar denominated assets liquid and thus attractive so inflowing money holds up the value of the US dollar that might otherwise be depressed by the twin deficits as Robert Triffin had famously predicted back in the late 1950s. (Desai 2013, Desai and Hudson 2021).

China's role vis-à-vis this system is widely misunderstood. In the vast academic industry devoted to talking up the US dollar system, China is generally portrayed as upholding this system thanks to its large dollar reserves. Many claim that China's reserve dollar holdings are what keeps the dollar system working.

However, not only are these holdings in decline, having now gone below Japan's holdings by a considerable margin; and not only are foreign holdings of US treasuries only about a third of all holdings of US treasuries, most of which are held by US public and private institutions and individuals; Chinese dollar reserves, all foreign dollar reserves and even all holdings of US treasuries are small fractions of the astronomical capital flows that actually hold up the dollar system.

These flows come from private and institutional investors in jurisdictions that have low or no capital controls. Most of them are from other rich, mostly Western, countries, as they were when the housing and credit bubbles of the 2000s were inflated. That is why these countries, chiefly the US, UK and Europe, suffered most as a result of that crisis and why it's more accurate to call it not the 'Global Financial Crisis' given that neither the participants nor the victims were 'global' but rather the North Atlantic Financial Crisis. Nevertheless, the wealthy and financial institutions in the rest of the world also participate in this system. They hail from countries whose financial systems have been reoriented away from the sort of development that can increase social productive capacities and towards the sort of comprador arrangements which keep the vast majority of society poor while allowing a small elite that exploits them to further speculate in the US dollar denominated financial system. Given its more or less complete disconnection from any productive investment whatsoever, this system is really little more than a giant casino.

China's financial system is not only disconnected from this casino, it is an instance of the opposite system. To understand this, we need to appreciate the evolution of China's financial system. Well into the reform period, Western analysts considered China's financial system – essentially its banking system given that asset markets were largely non-existent until recently – to be near insolvent. Today, however, China is home to three of the world's five biggest banks enjoying a remarkably low rate of non-performing loans (Williams, 2020, 1-2.).

This is not the result, as much Western scholarship imagines, of the neoliberal reform of Chinese finance. The mainstream of Western scholarship and Western oriented scholarship in China judge the Chinese financial system 'according to the degree of implementation of free market policies' (Williams 2017, 3). What implementing the full paraphernalia of neoliberal financialisation would involve can be briefly listed: central bank independence (which, in reality, means regulatory capture of the regulators by the regulated), private ownership of financial institutions, stock and other financial and real asset markets, unrestricted foreign ownership, and greater 'financial inclusion' (which means, in reality, indebting anyone who can be gainfully indebted). Little of this literature appreciates the extensive damage done by the Western system both to its home economies and to those abroad (Byrd 1983 is an early example while Amstad et al 2020 is a more recent one).

For instance, Walter and Howie praise the reforms that culminated in China's entry into the World Trade Organisation (WTO) and criticise limitations and reversals. The resulting financial system, they say, is still largely confined to banks, with underdeveloped asset markets. It underserves 'China's heroic savers', with low interest rates. Since China's large banks typically focus on financing the state-owned and/or closely influenced and supervised corporations that remain at the commanding heights of China's economy, it leaves many smaller businesses without any reliable source of capital. Not only do Walter and Howie fault the Chinese government for protecting this system from competition or failure, particularly by keeping foreign banks confined to a marginal role, overall, they complain further that

> Beyond the pressures of competition, the Party treats its banks as basic utilities that provide unlimited capital to the cherished state-owned enterprises. With all aspects of banking under the Party's control, risk is thought to be manageable. Even so, at the end of each of the last three decades, these banks have faced virtual, if not actual, bankruptcy, surviving only because they have had the full, unstinting, and costly support of the Party. (Walter and Howie 2012, 27)

These 'virtual' bankruptcies were, according to Walter and Howie, solved by the "traditional problem-solving approach of simply shifting money from one pocket to another and letting time and fading memory do the rest". Western financial institutions also generate similar criticisms: a chapter of a World Bank report on the Chinese economy for instance, later redacted under Chinese government protest, "gave warning that 'the poor performance of the financial system' had confirmed previous assessments that the system was "unbalanced, repressed, costly to maintain and potentially unstable"' (Donnan and Wildau 2015).

Indeed, these Western criticisms ignore many rather obvious facts. First, while asset markets may indeed be less developed in China, stock markets have rarely provided long term patient capital, hype about 'venture capital' notwithstanding. That is why the industrially and productively most successful countries have financial systems where banks provide the patient capital industry needs. Moreover, in so far as stock markets are developing in China, they are being oriented and regulated to direct savings towards high-priority sectors and enterprises. Secondly, on the matter of high(er) interest rates, it is widely understood that they strangle industry. In so far as the needs of savers are concerned, they are better served by public services

PATIENT FINANCE: BEIJING'S CORE CHALLENGE TO WASHINGTON

that obviate the need for ordinary people to keep high savings. Thirdly, as far as small businesses are concerned, their need for capital of the right – long-term and patient – sort will likely require the expansion of China's financial system on its present basis downwards into the economy, not its neoliberal reform.

Above all, such Western observers are surely wrong when they claim that the 'shifting from one pocket to another' cannot go on forever and that some day, in Walter and Howie's words, when, "[t]ied up as it is in financial knots, the system's size, scale, and access to seemingly limitless capital can [no longer] solve the problems of the banks", the system will succumb to further market reforms abandoned after 2005. The traditional problem solving approach of shifting money from one pocket to another has always been the way to deal with banking crises in any context. After all, banking always relies on judgments that are bound to prove mistaken now and then. The real question is whether the 'shifting money', in other words, bailout, protects the productive or the financial sector, and whether it protects ordinary people, their savings or employment or the elites and their fortunes.

The simple fact is that Western countries have bailed out their banks just as regularly but have done so in doubly destructive ways. On the one hand, the beneficiaries of the bailouts have typically been the very financial institutions which inflated the bubble with their reckless speculation in the first place, not the ordinary people who became their unwitting victims. On the other, the bailout became necessary thanks to socially, economically and politically destructive asset bubbles inflated by reckless institutions, not for patient productive investment as, on occasion, may have happened in China.

To understand the Chinese system, we need to understand it historically and in relation to the very different role that the Chinese banking system has played in China's economy and its impressive expansion of recent years.

China's banking system was long dominated by a single bank, the People's Bank of China. After the official adoption of a socialist market economy in the early 1990s, market reforms were gradually introduced to liberalise it considerably (for the early history see Jiang and Yao 2017. 15-20). However, contrary to western views, this liberalisation has not aimed at creating China's version of today's neoliberal Western banks. To be sure, reformers have learned and borrowed a great deal from Western banking techniques and institutions as they introduced competition, reduced the inevitable moral hazard in a system ultimately protected by the state, allowed carefully calibrated private ownership, including foreign shareholding, and imposed prudential limits on lending and risk-taking (Jiang and Yao 2017, 35-38).

However, reformers have proceeded with caution, bearing in mind the Chinese adage about 'crossing the river by feeling the stones'. Their policy and technical borrowings from the West have been governed by the authorities' aims, usually articulated as principles arising from an understanding of China's economic needs and history. Reform has sought to 'transform the banking system to a market-oriented one that is viable in the long run thereby better serving the economic development of the country' (Jiang and Yao 2017, 55), that is, serving the needs of the productive economy rather than of a tiny financial elite (Williams 2020). Unlike the neoliberal financialised banking systems, China's banks have played a critical role in maintaining the remarkably high investment rate that has been so critical to China's economic success (Ross 2020).

This has been accomplished by ensuring that banking is regulated in accordance with the party's goals for the productive economy, that is to say, in the clear political interest of the vast majority of Chinese people, not by some putatively 'independent' central bank which is actually run in the interest of a tiny financial and investor elite. The suspension of the Ant Group's initial public offering and other run-ins of China's big corporations with the government demonstrate that this principle has not been suspended and the current US economic aggression towards China will put a greater premium on steady industrial growth, which requires finance to be more like China's than the US's (with many even in the US speaking of the need for industrial policy). When the Ant Group tried to defy Beijing's tougher prudential requirements for consumer lending by going ahead with its IPO, it was called on the carpet and the IPO had to be suspended abruptly. It was an instance of Beijing reining in the political power of defiant capitalists as well as opposing any trend towards profit-driven expansion of consumer borrowing (Kynge et al 2020) that detracts from the productive focus of the financial system. Given its commitment to raising wages, the last thing China needs is consumer credit to replace low wages and preparing the ground for mass destitution as happened in the US after the 2008 crash. Regulators are also wary of financialisation lowering growth.

Will the Renminbi replace the Dollar? Can it? Should it?

Like the Chinese financial system, the internationalisation of the Renminbi is also found wanting against the benchmark of the unstable, predatory and volatile dollar system (Cohen 2015, Prasad 2017 and Guo et al 2020 are typical works). The dominant claim here is that the renminbi is not being internationalised on the pattern of the dollar – whether because the government is unable or unwilling to do so – and so the dollar's position is secure.

Benjamin Cohen, for instance, assuming that currency internationalisation on the dollar pattern is desirable in itself, finds that Beijing's internationalising ambitions are checked by episodes like the outflow of nearly a trillion dollars in 2015 that forced devaluation (McDowell 2019, 194) and by the fear that it will undermine the party's political hold. Thus, Cohen concludes that the dollar remains "the *indispensable currency* – the one money the world cannot do without" thanks to the 'depth of US financial markets' (Cohen 2015, 6) along with "still broad network externalities in trade, a wide range of political ties, and vast military reach". While acknowledging some progress in the internationalisation of the renminbi, particularly along the trade track, he concludes that further progress is doubtful.

Thus the renminbi will not replace the dollar: "On its own the gravitational pull of China's economic size will not suffice. Other factors – above all, *a well-developed and open financial structure* – must also come into play" and China is unlikely to be willing to engage in the necessary financial liberalisation because it would entail "a significant modification of Beijing's authoritarian economic model" (Cohen, 236, emphasis added). Of course, what Cohen calls 'authoritarian' about China's economy is precisely the lack of complete freedom of capital, which is, in fact, the secret of China's success. And the limits to the internationalisation of the renminbi are placed precisely by China's economic success: to sustain it, it is critically important that China avoid the archaic, short term, speculative and predatory financial systems sported by the US and the UK. Adopting it would bring an end to the spectacular growth China has experienced precisely because it is home to a contrasting financial system. Interestingly, in the US, since at least the 2008 financial crisis, critical voices pointing to the costs the US itself has had to pay for its financialised dollar internationalisation are becoming louder (Bergsten, 2009, 2011). Indeed, financial systems of the finance capital type have historically been reluctant to internationalise their currencies in the same manner (see, for instance, Henning 1994, Helleiner and Malkin 2012, for a useful overview, see Chey and Li) for good reason.

As we have seen, however, much of this is beside the point. The dollar has pushed the contradictions of national money posing as world money to its limits. Its end, when it comes, will be the result of its own contradictions, not because a 'successor' has emerged (see Desai and Hudson 2021). The renminbi is certainly not going to follow in its footsteps. US authorities had already overestimated the dollar's prospects when they blocked multilateral agreements creating an International Clearing Union and Bancor as Keynes originally proposed at Bretton Woods (Desai 2009). Only such arrangements can create a stable and viable world money capable of serving the needs of productive economies in a multipolar world, not the currency of any single country, no matter how powerful.

Given that Western recalcitrance is unlikely to permit this in the short or medium term, regional, bi- and multi-lateral agreements will be the realistic options. The reality is that the internationalisation of the renminbi is proceeding according to the domestic and international needs of China's productive economy and it is likely to proceed further along the same path. It is, however, radically different from that taken by the dollar today or even sterling in the past. This is precisely the form that is the foundation of its attractiveness to the developing world. There is certainly no evidence that China's leadership is willing to tread the path of the dollar: the cost to its productive system would be too high.

Will China's property sector crash, taking the economy with it?

Given the differences between the Chinese and Western financial systems, while undoubtedly Chinese asset and property prices have risen in recent years and are now in decline, it is unlikely, as many fear (Song and Xiong 2018), that China will suffer the bursting of a property bubble and, as Walden Bello fears, also suffer an aftermath of decades of Japan or US-like economic stagnation.

Bello contends that though workers complain of unaffordable housing, authorities are loath to end the bubble given that "China's real-estate sector accounts for an estimated 15 percent of gross domestic product (GDP) and 20 percent of the national demand for loans". Shutting down this economic engine is not done lightly (Bello, 4). Surprisingly for a critical writer, Bello fingers financial repression as the chief culprit. According to him, low returns on savers' deposits leads them to speculate in assets and the financial system's focus on large, state-owned and export-oriented enterprises leads investors to the property market and to the pervasive shadow banking system. Only "a fundamental reform in the country's national credit system to end the virtual monopoly by the export oriented economic complex of the banking system", which creates the "strong demand for these *sub rosa* entities" (Bello, 6) can resolve the problem. He also blames the 'export lobby' for hijacking the 2008 stimulus "that had been intended to place money and resources in the hands of consumers" and for preventing further liberalisation which would end financial repression and orient the financial sector towards financing small investors and firms producing for the domestic market (Bello, 180).

However, there are at least three major problems with this diagnosis. Firstly, rather than further inflating a property bubble in the interests of economic growth, not only have the authorities been clear that houses are for living, not speculation, they have also managed the decline in property prices. Secondly, in naturalising savers' search for high returns, it fails to see that the real solution to that lies in covering gaps in social provision that really lie behind households' high savings, and the authorities are already engaged in this. Thirdly, in framing the export sector as the culprit, critics ignore the extent to which, since 2008, the Chinese economy, never as reliant on exports as was widely believed anyway, was reorienting toward domestic investment and consumption, a development that has culminated in the 'Dual Circulation' strategy, emphasising an increasing importance of the domestic market as a growth stimulant (Tang 2020). Finally, by blaming financial repression, Bello appears to be implying that China's financial system should become more like the speculative western one.

Undoubtedly some developers had behaved irresponsibly and they are being wound up or restructured, with the authorities seeking a new model of real estate development. As for the banking system, sober observers, even Western ones, reject alarmism. Acknowledging that some Chinese banks, particularly regional ones, are in trouble thanks to their involvement in the real estate market, they caution against interpreting these troubles "as indications of an imminent financial crisis". Chinese authorities are approaching the problem through a pincer movement. They are at once putting pressure on banks to "clean up their balance sheets, raise new capital, and dispose of bad loans" and lending "to struggling companies at nonmarket rates to forestall a further slowdown in the pace of economic growth". This indicates that the "PBOC and the CPC leadership remain committed to ensuring stability. Authorities have so far successfully contained isolated bank failures and prevented sector-wide contagion" (Bisio et al, 19). Finally, the authorities are protecting ordinary people by encouraging the completion of units already paid for and expanding social provision of housing, including through state purchase of excess units.

In conclusion, China's financial system is a standing indictment of the Western one and there are no indications that it is about to give up the massive advantages of its financial system and opt for the Western neoliberal model, not even for the poisoned chalice of a world role for the renminbi. On the contrary, to continue along the path of developing socialism, it is more likely to develop the productive elements, as part of a long-term strategy aimed at achieving common prosperity. As it does, China's financial system will remain the most powerful challenge to the Washington consensus.

REFERENCES

Amstad, Marlene, Guofeng Sun and Wei Xiong (eds). 2020. The Handbook of China's Financial System. Princeton NJ: Princeton University Press.
Bello, Walden. 2019. *Paper Dragons: China and the Next Crash*. London: Zed.

Bergsten, Fred. 2009. 'The Dollar and the Deficits: How Washington Can Prevent the Next Crisis'. *Foreign Affairs*, November/December, Vol. 88, no. 6, pp. 20-38.

Bisio, Virgilio. 2020. 'China's Banking Sector Risks and Implications for the United States'. Staff Research Report, Washington, DC: US-China Economic and Security Commission. https://www.uscc.gov/research/chinas-banking-sector-risks-and-implications-united-states

Byrd, W., 1983. *China's financial system*. London: Routledge,

Chey, Hyoung-Kyu and Yu Wai Vic Li. 2020. 'Chinese Domestic Politics and the Internationalisation of the Renminbi'. *Political Science Quarterly*, 135/1, 37-65.

Cohen, Benjamin, *Currency Power: Understanding Monetary Rivalry*. Princeton, Princeton University Pres, 2015.

Desai, Radhika. 2009. "Keynes Redux: From World Money to International Money at Last?" Wayne Anthony and Julie Guard eds. *Bailouts and Bankruptcies*. Halifax: Fernwood Books.

_____. 2013. *Geopolitical Economy: After US Hegemony, Globalization and Empire*. London: Pluto.

_____. 2018.'John Maynard Pangloss: *Indian Currency and Finance* in Imperial Context' in Sheila Dow, Jesper Jespersen & Geoff Tily (eds), *The General Theory and Keynes for the 21st Century, Cheltenham*: Edward Elgar Publishing Ltd, 2018, pages 116-131.

Desai, Radhika and Michael Hudson. 2021. 'Beyond the Dollar Creditocracy: A Geopolitical Economy', *Valdai Club Paper* No. 116. Moscow: Valdai Club. With Michael Hudson. 7 July 2021, https://valdaiclub.com/a/valdai-papers/valdai-papers-116/

Donnan, Shawn and Gabriel Wildau. 2015. World Bank denies China sought to have critical report censored', *Financial Times*, 3 July. https://www.ft.com/content/5bc2d58c-21c2-11e5-aa5a-398b2169cf79

Ferguson, Niall and Moritz Schularick. 2007. 'Chimerica' and the Global Asset Market Boom'. *International Finance* 10:3, 2007: pp. 215–239.

Guo, Kai, Ningxin Jiang, Fan Qi and Yue Zhao. 2020. 'RMB Internationalization' in Marlene Amstad, Guofeng Sun, and Wei Xiong, *The Handbook of China's Financial System*, Princeton, NJ: Princeton University Press.

Helleiner, Eric and Anton Malkin. 2012. 'Sectoral Interests and Global Money: Renminbi, Dollar and the Domestic Foundations of International Currency Policy'. *Open Economic Review* 23, 33-55.

Henning, C. Randall. 1994. *Currencies and Politics in the United States, Germany, and Japan*. Washington, DC: Institute for International Economics.

Hilferding, Rudolf. 1910/1981. *Finance Capital: A Study of the Latest Phase of Capitalist Development*. Edited with an Introduction by Tom Bottomore, Tr. Morris Watnick and Sam Gordon, London: Routledge.

Jiang, Chunxia and Shijie Yao. 2017. *Chinese Banking Reform: From the Pre-WTO Period to the Financial Crisis and Beyond*. The Nottingham China Policy Institute Series. London: Palgrave Macmillan.

Kotz, David M and Fred Weir. 1997. *Revolution from Above: The Demise of the Soviet System*. London: Routledge.

Kynge, J. Sender, H., and Yu, S., 2020. 'The Party is pushing back': Why Beijing reined in Jack Ma and Ant. *Financial Times*, November 4. Available at: www.ft.com/content/3d2f174d-aa73-44fc-8c90-45c2a554e97b [Issued March 25, 2021].

Marx, Karl. 1894/1981. Karl Marx, *Capital* , Volume III. London: Penguin.

McDowell, Daniel.2019. 'From tailwinds to headwinds: The Troubled Internationalization of the Renminbi'. *Handbook on the International Political Economy of China*, edited by Ka Zeng, Cheltenham: Edward Elgar.

Prasad, Eswar. 2017. *Gaining Currency: The Rise of the Renminbi*. Oxford: Oxford University Press.

Rohatyn, Felix. 1994. "World Capital: The Needs and the Risks". *New York Review of Books,* July 14.

Ross, John. 2020. 'Why China maintained its strong economic growth'.

LearningfromChina.net, https://www.learningfromchina.net/why-china-maintained-its-strong-economic-growth/.

Song, Z., and W. Xiong (2018). "Risks in China's Financial System." *Annual Review of Financial Economics.* 10: 261–86.Shaw, Timothy. 1983. 'Debates about Africa's future: The Brandt, World Bank and Lagos plan blueprints'. *Third World Quarterly*, Vol. 5, No. 2, Africa: Tensions and Contentions, pp. 330-344.

Tang, Frank. 2020. 'What is China's Dual Circulation and Why is it important'. *South China Morning Post.* 19 November. https://www.scmp.com/economy/china-economy/article/3110184/what-chinas-dual-circulation-economic-strategy-and-why-it Toussaint, Eric. 2020. 'The World Bank saw the debt crisis looming'. Committee for the Abolition of Illegitimate Debt (CADTM)

Tsang, Steve. 2016. 'Consolidating Political and Governance Strength' in S. Tsang and H. Men (eds) *China in the Xi Jinping Era.* Nottingham; School of Contemporary Chinese Studies, The Nottingham China Policy Institute Series.

Walter, Carl and Fraser Howie. 2012. *Red Capitalism: The Fragile Financial Foundations of China's Extraordinary Rise* Wiley

Williams, Guy. *The Evolution of China's Banking System, 1993-2017.* London: Routledge, 2020

Wang, Bijun and Kailin Gao. 2019. 'Forty Years' of China's Outward Foreign Direct Investment: Retrospect and Challenges Ahead'. *China and the World Economy* 27/3, pp. 1-24.

Wolf, Martin. 2014. 'Holdouts give vultures a bad name'. *Financial Times.* 2 September. https://www.ft.com/content/bf3bd3f2-31ef-11e4-b929-00144feabdc0

11

How China survived the end of history

Carlos Martinez

> What's going on in other countries is not our business, but we should make one thing clear: in China socialism will not change. China will surely follow to the end the socialist road it has chosen. No one will be able to overwhelm us. As long as China doesn't collapse, one fifth of the world's population will be upholding socialism. We are full of confidence that socialism has a bright future. (Deng Xiaoping)[1]

The Soviet Union ceased to exist on the 26th of December 1991 – a tragic day in the history of the global working class. In the ensuing four years, Russian life expectancy fell from 65 to 57 – unprecedented in times of peace. The previously impressive healthcare infrastructure collapsed and the peoples of the former Soviet Union were subjected to epidemics of poverty-fuelled diseases not seen for many decades.

The tragedy reverberated globally. As Fidel Castro noted:

> the destruction of socialism in the USSR ... inflicted terrible damage on all peoples of the world and created a bad situation for the Third World in particular.[2]

In the same period, between 1989 and 1991, there were counter-revolutions in the German Democratic Republic, Hungary, Romania, Bulgaria, Poland, Czechoslovakia and Albania. These countries left socialism behind, overwhelmingly joined the Washington Consensus, and largely aligned themselves with the neoliberal nineties.

The collapse of the Soviet Union and European socialism could reasonably be described as the worst defeat suffered by the global working class in its history. It gave a lifeline to imperialism and set back the cause of human liberation by decades.

Many assumed that People's China and the other remaining socialist states – Cuba, Vietnam, Laos and the Democratic People's Republic of Korea (DPRK) – would follow the same miserable path. Capitalist ideologues proclaimed the "end of history" and told us that China's integration into the US-led neoliberal-imperialist world order was a matter of "when", not "if".

Among the Western left there were those offering similar predictions, albeit with a sprinkling of Marxist phraseology: China's economic reform was essentially a project of capitalist restoration, which would inevitably lead to the consolidation of political power in the group of people that own and deploy capital.

Over three decades later, these predictions – utopian dreams of the right, dystopian nightmares of the left – have failed to materialise. The People's Republic of China is very much a going concern. Living standards have increased dramatically; extreme poverty has been eliminated; China has become a global leader in science and technology; it leads the way in addressing the climate crisis; Chinese society is highly stable; and the government enjoys an outstanding level of popularity and legitimacy. China is suffering neither stagnation, despite the best efforts of the advocates of a 'new Cold War', nor isolation – indeed today it is the largest trading partner of two-thirds of the world's countries.

And of course, China's flag stays red. As General Secretary Xi Jinping puts it:

> Socialism with Chinese characteristics is pure socialism and nothing else. The basic principles of scientific socialism must not be abandoned; otherwise it is not socialism. What doctrine a country may choose is based on whether it can resolve the historical problems that confront that country. Both history and reality have shown us that only socialism can save China and only socialism with Chinese characteristics can bring development to China. This conclusion is the result of historical exploration, and the choice of the people.[3]

This chapter seeks to shine some light on how China has been able to survive. Why has China's process of Reform and Opening Up, initiated in 1978, had such wildly different outcomes to Mikhail Gorbachev's *perestroika* (restructuring) and *glasnost* (openness)?

Economic stagnation versus economic miracle

> The vastly different results of the Russian and Chinese reforms are demonstrative of the critical importance of choosing the right reform strategies and paths. (Hu Angang)[4]

Contrary to popular prejudice, the centrally-planned economy was, at least in its early stages, extraordinarily successful in both the Soviet Union and China. The Soviet Union – a predominantly rural, technologically backward, poorly educated country – was transformed into a modern industrial economy with a high level of education and an advanced urban infrastructure; a world power capable of defeating the Nazi war machine. Unemployment was essentially non-existent, and the quality of state-provided services such as education and healthcare was world-class.

It is highly unlikely that any other economic model would have allowed such rapid development; certainly no capitalist economic programme has brought about large-scale industrialisation in so short a period of time. Prominent economist Ha-Joon Chang writes:

> To everyone's surprise, the early Soviet industrialisation was a big success, most graphically proven by its ability to repel the Nazi advance on the Eastern Front during the Second World War. Income per capita is estimated to have grown at 5 percent per year between 1928 and 1938 – an astonishingly rapid rate in a world in which income typically grew at 1-2 per cent per year.[5]

Even Henry Kissinger was moved to declare in 1960 that:

> starting from a position of substantial inferiority in almost all areas, the Soviet Union has caught up with and surpassed us in more categories than are comforting.[6]

Similarly in China, in the initial decades of socialist construction, the country was transformed beyond recognition. Feudalism was dismantled and the country was industrialised. Land was irrigated; cities grew rapidly; new industrial hubs were established; railways and roads spread across the country; and output increased massively. From being one of the poorest and most technologically backward countries in the world, China developed a broad science and technology infrastructure, one notable success of which was the successful testing of an atomic bomb in 1964.

Nevertheless, experience in the Soviet Union, China and elsewhere indicated that a fully-planned and centralised economy was subject to the law of diminishing returns. As Michael Parenti puts it, this model "was useful and even necessary in the earlier period of siege socialism to produce steel, wheat and tanks in order to build an industrial base and withstand the Nazi onslaught"; yet in a post-war environment with changing needs and a far more complex product mix, the Soviet system "eventually hindered technological development and growth, and proved incapable of supplying a wide-enough range of consumer goods and services".[7] By the early 1970s, the economic gap between the socialist countries and the capitalist countries was starting to widen again. In terms of GDP, the Soviet economy peaked at 44 percent of the US's GDP in 1970, and by 1989 it was 36 percent.[8]

The Italian philosopher Domenico Losurdo writes that, after the period of frenetic building of socialism, followed by World War 2, followed by reconstruction, came

> the transition from great historical crisis to a more 'normal' period" in which "the masses' enthusiasm and commitment to production and work weakened and then disappeared.

In its final few years, Losurdo argues:

> the Soviet Union was characterised by massive absenteeism and disengagement in the workplace: not only did production development stagnate, but there was no longer any application of the principle that Marx said drove socialism — remuneration according to the quantity and quality of work delivered.[9]

The British journalist Kate Clark, who had been *Morning Star* correspondent in Moscow in the 1980s, writes that, when she first visited the Soviet Union in the 1960s, "enthusiasm and belief in the system, in socialism, was still widespread and undeniable." However, by the 1980s, "for many the flame of that new socialist society, with all that it was meant to bring, started guttering in the hearts of many ordinary people". Workers often felt indifferent to their work. The economy "could not absorb and develop new ideas and techniques", since "the success of an individual enterprise was judged, not by new inventions or innovations, but by whether or not it fulfilled its plan, handed down to it from Gosplan (the state planning committee)".[10]

By the 1970s, China was facing similar problems. It had made incredible, unprecedented progress in terms of life expectancy, land ownership, social equality and education in the first decades following the founding of the People's Republic in 1949. It had ended famine for the first time in China's history. It probably had the greatest level of equality of any country in the world. Nonetheless, it was still a long way from being an advanced country. Hundreds of millions of people in the villages faced food insecurity and poor housing conditions.

Losurdo writes that China in the late 1970s:

> resembled the Soviet Union to an extraordinary degree in its last years of existence: the socialist principle of compensation based on the amount and quality of work delivered was substantially liquidated, and disaffection, disengagement, absenteeism and anarchy reigned in the workplace.[11]

In China as in the Soviet Union, people's expectations for a better life increasingly weren't being met, and this was impacting popular confidence in the superiority of the socialist system. Cut off from the global division of labour, it was not able to quickly learn from others or benefit from the emerging wave of automation and digitisation. There was a shortage of capital, a relatively low level of technological development compared to the imperialist powers, and a lack of incentives for production and innovation.

The key insight of the CPC leadership in the late 1970s was that legitimacy of the socialist system would only be maintained by eliminating poverty and improving people's living conditions, and that this could only be achieved through a process of rapid modernisation and development of the productive forces. Deng Xiaoping explained that economic development was particularly important in the light of fast growth in other East and Southeast Asian countries:

> The economies of some of our neighbouring countries and regions are growing faster than ours. If our economy stagnates or develops only slowly, the people will make comparisons and ask why.[12]

Superficially, the reform strategy pursued by China from 1978 shares some similarities with the various attempts at economic reform in the Soviet Union, particularly the set of policies introduced by the Gorbachev leadership under the umbrella of *perestroika*. However, there are profound differences between the Chinese and Soviet approaches that help to explain the unquestionable success of one and the comprehensive failure of the other.

China's approach to reform was extremely cautious and pragmatic, "based on a step-by-step, piecemeal and experimental approach. If a reform worked it was extended to new areas; if it failed then it was abandoned."[13] All reforms had to be tested in practice, all results had to be analysed, and all analysis had to inform future experiments. Chen Yun, one of the key architects of the economic reform, stated in 1980 that:

> the steps must be steady, because we shall encounter many complicated problems. So do not rush... We should proceed

with experiments, review our experience from time to time, and correct mistakes whenever we discover them, so that minor mistakes will not grow into major ones.[14]

Many key reform concepts came from the grassroots. "We processed their ideas and raised them to the level of guidelines for the whole country. Practice is the sole criterion for testing truth."[15] Peasants were allowed to sell a proportion of their produce on the market, thereby creating a direct financial incentive to produce more. Areas of the economy – particularly in the service sector and light industry – were opened up to non-state businesses, usually in the form of town or village-based collectives. Prices of certain commodities were liberalised so as to attract capital to areas with high demand. Foreign investment was encouraged.

Reform in China was patient, incremental and results-oriented, whereas "Gorbachev made the fatal mistake of trying to do too much, too fast."[16] Gorbachev's reforms were implemented in a heavy-handed, top-down way, without leveraging the ideas and creativity of the masses or attempting to collate feedback. Given that the project was presented as a form of 'democratisation', it's ironic that it was carried out in a profoundly undemocratic manner. The leadership didn't mobilise the existing, proven structures of society, but sought to bypass and weaken them.

China relaxed restrictions on private capital, but it didn't take the nuclear option that Gorbachev did of dismantling the state planning agencies overnight. Rather, "the relaxation of restrictions on private capital development was combined with state control and planned and state-led heavy investment."[17] Indeed the state-owned enterprises continued to get stronger, the commanding heights of the economy were maintained (and are still maintained) under state control, and the system of planning was kept in place and improved. The whole reform process has been carried out under the control of the government and has taken place within the context of an overall planned economy.

By 1991, the last year of the USSR's existence, the Soviet economy was contracting at a rate of 15 percent per year. Investment collapsed. Homelessness and grinding poverty emerged for the first time since World War 2. *Perestroika* turned a sluggish economy into a failing one. In China meanwhile, living standards have improved beyond recognition. Per capita GDP was $200 in 1978; by 2023 it had reached $12,750. The number of people living in absolute poverty (as defined by the World Bank) has fallen from 840 million to zero. Wages have increased continuously.

Although inequality has emerged as a serious problem, practically all Chinese people are substantially better off than they were 45 years ago in terms of nutrition, housing, clothing, access to services, and ability to travel. Consumer goods that were previously considered luxuries – such as washing machines, refrigerators, heated shower units, air conditioners, televisions, computers – can be found in almost every home.

Human Development Index (HDI) is a compound metric that incorporates life expectancy, educational level and per capita income. In HDI terms, China has risen from 0.407 in 1980 to 0.788 in 2022. It is the only country to have moved from the *low* to the *high* HDI category – leap-frogging *medium* – since the UN Development Program (UNDP) first began studying global HDI trends in 1990.[18]

Whereas Soviet infrastructure was starting to crumble by the 1980s, modern Chinese infrastructure is world-class. Indeed, the quality of roads, trains, airports, ports and buildings in major Chinese cities is now considerably superior to affluent Western cities such as London and New York.

The success of China's reforms, and the failure of the Soviet ones, is surely a crucial factor in explaining why People's China still exists and the Soviet Union does not.

Politics in command

There are also important political factors to address, principal among which is that China is not weakening Communist Party rule or attacking its own history.

The CPC leadership was clear about this from the start, with Deng Xiaoping commenting that:

> Western countries want to bring about the peaceful evolution of socialist countries towards capitalism… If China allowed bourgeois liberalisation, there would inevitably be turmoil. We would accomplish nothing, and our principles, policies, line and development strategy would all be doomed to failure.[19]

In the Soviet Union, economic reform was accompanied by a concerted attempt to undermine the legitimacy of the Communist Party and the confidence of the people in their history. Gorbachev's team developed the idea of *glasnost* – 'openness' – to encapsulate policies of greater government transparency, wider political discussion and increased popular participation. While such goals sounded unobjectionable, indeed laudable, the real objective of the campaign was to empower those sections of Soviet society that were enthusiastic about Gorbachev's economic proposals: predominantly pro-Western liberals and people who were starting to make money in newly-opened markets or the already existing 'black markets'. Empowering these people meant working to erode the Communist Party's leading role in the government. Glasnost thus became a vehicle for an all-out attack on the legitimacy of rule by the working class, with its concentrated expression in the leading role of the communist party, and ultimately provided a powerful weapon for an anti-communist constituency – people who wanted to overthrow Soviet socialism.

Prominent Chinese academics Cheng Enfu and Liu Zixu observe:

> In the name of promoting young cadres and of reform, Gorbachev replaced large numbers of party, political and military leaders with anti-CPSU and anti-socialist cadres or cadres with ambivalent positions. This practice laid the foundations, in organisational and cadre selection terms, for the political 'shift of direction.'[20]

Yegor Ligachev, a high-ranking Soviet official who witnessed all this first hand, supports this conclusion:

> What happened in our country is primarily the result of the debilitation and eventual elimination of the Communist Party's leading role in society, the ejection of the party from major policymaking, its ideological and organisational unravelling.[21]

The political transformation was supported by a thoroughgoing media campaign denigrating Soviet history, vastly exaggerating the excesses and mistakes of the Stalin period, and even attacking the Soviet Union's role in the Second World War. Kate Clark comments that"

> the leadership's questioning of every facet of society over the previous seventy years, from centralised planning to historical events, and from collectivised agriculture to parliamentary structures, had undermined many citizens' faith in their system.[22]

It should be noted that the foundations for Gorbachev's anti-communist propaganda campaign had been laid decades earlier, when Nikita Khrushchev issued his famous 'secret speech' denouncing Stalin, in one fell swoop "casting a god into hell" and, in so doing, delegitimising the extraordinary achievements of the Communist Party of the Soviet Union and the Soviet people up to that point.[23] While a critical examination of aspects of the Stalin period may have been necessary, Khrushchev's denunciation was so exaggerated and unbalanced as to substantially impact the Soviet ideological consensus, prompting Deng Xiaoping to later remark:

> We will forever keep Chairman Mao's portrait on Tiananmen Gate as a symbol of our country, and we will always

remember him as a founder of our Party and state… We will not do to Chairman Mao what Khrushchev did to Stalin."[24]

During the glasnost period, the 'reassessment' of Soviet history went so far that Cuban leader Fidel Castro was moved to comment:

> Without a strong, disciplined and respected party, it's impossible to develop a revolution or a truly socialist rectification. It isn't possible to carry out such a process by slandering socialism, destroying its values, discrediting the party, demoralising the vanguard, renouncing its leading role, ending social discipline, sowing chaos and anarchy all around. This might foster a counter-revolution, but not revolutionary changes… It's repugnant that many in the USSR itself are dedicating themselves to destroying the historic feats and extraordinary merits of that heroic people.[25]

In 1990, the Soviet constitution was amended, removing the reference to the CPSU as "the leading and guiding force of the Soviet society and the nucleus of its political system", thereby paving the way for a Western-style multi-party system.

The Communist Party had been the major vehicle for promoting the needs and ideas of the Soviet working class; once it was sidelined, the workers had no obvious means of organising in defence of their interests. Meanwhile, in a context where a pro-capitalist minority was building up its economic strength, the supposedly democratic reforms allowed this emerging class to translate money into political power.

The Chinese leadership, in contrast, has always understood that the People's Republic of China could not survive without the continued leadership of the Communist Party; this is a key lesson learned from the collapse of the Soviet Union. In practically every important speech on China's development path from 1978 until his death in 1997, Deng Xiaoping insisted on what he termed the Four Cardinal Principles: 1) Defend the socialist path; 2) Maintain the dictatorship of the proletariat (working class rule); 3) Maintain the leadership of the party; and 4) Adhere to Marxism-Leninism and Mao Zedong Thought. He was extremely clear regarding the importance of a workers' state:

> What kind of democracy do the Chinese people need today? It can only be socialist democracy, people's democracy, and not bourgeois democracy… Personal interests must be subordinated to collective ones, the interests of the part to those of the whole, and immediate to long-term interests. In other words, limited interests must be subordinated to

overall interests, and minor interests to major ones... It is still necessary to exercise dictatorship over all these anti-socialist elements... The fact of the matter is that socialism cannot be defended or built up without the dictatorship of the proletariat.[26]

The CPC has not followed the Soviet example of attacking its own history. Xi Jinping observes that:

one important reason for the disintegration of the Soviet Union and the collapse of the CPSU is the complete denial of the history of the Soviet Union, and the history of the CPSU, the denial of Lenin and other leading personalities, and historical nihilism confused the people's thoughts.[27]

Although the post-Mao Chinese leadership made serious criticisms of certain policies, it has never come anywhere close to repudiating Mao and undermining the basic ideological and historical foundations of Chinese socialism. No 'Chinese Wall' has been constructed between the Mao-era and the post-Mao era; the two phases are inextricably linked, and are both considered as "pragmatic explorations in building socialism conducted by the people under the leadership of the Party."[28]

Compare Gorbachev's clumsy historical assessment of the Soviet Union with the words of Xi Jinping on the centenary of the Communist Party of China:

We owe all that we have achieved over the past hundred years to the concerted efforts of the Chinese Communists, the Chinese people, and the Chinese nation. China's Communists, with Comrades Mao Zedong, Deng Xiaoping, Jiang Zemin and Hu Jintao as their chief representatives, have made tremendous and historic contributions to the rejuvenation of the Chinese nation. To them, we express our deepest respect.

Let us take this moment to cherish the memory of Comrades Mao Zedong, Zhou Enlai, Liu Shaoqi, Zhu De, Deng Xiaoping, Chen Yun, and other veteran revolutionaries who contributed greatly to China's revolution, construction, and reform, and to the founding, consolidation, and development of the Communist Party of China; let us cherish the memory of the revolutionary martyrs who bravely laid down their lives to establish, defend, and develop the People's Republic; let us cherish the memory of those who dedicated their lives to reform, opening up, and socialist modernisation; and let us cherish the memory of all the men and women who fought tenaciously for national independence and the liberation of the people in modern times. Their great contributions to our motherland and our nation will be immortalised in the annals of history, and their noble spirit will live on forever in the hearts of the Chinese people.[29]

The CPSU leadership suffered a crisis of legitimacy of its own creation. Gorbachev and his colleagues attacked and weakened the organs of working class rule. They colluded in the transfer of political power to anti-socialist forces. In China, however, as Martin Jacques points out:

> the rule of the Communist Party is no longer in doubt: it enjoys the prestige that one would expect given the transformation that it has presided over.[30]

China's adherence to socialist democracy and to Communist Party rule, and its continued upholding of Marxism and the history of the Chinese Revolution, have been crucial components of its success.

Peaceful development

From the very beginning – that is, from 1917 onwards – socialist states have had to deal with the question of relations with the imperialist world. Peaceful coexistence has been a necessity in a world where capitalism continues to dominate.

The Five Principles of Peaceful Coexistence, first put forward by Premier Zhou Enlai in 1954, recognise that states with different social systems – capitalist or socialist, imperialist or non-imperialist – will very likely continue to exist for an extended period and therefore must be able to coexist without descending into potentially devastating war.

Although the US imposed a total blockade on China shortly after the establishment of the People's Republic in 1949, the Chinese leadership's preference was always for peaceful coexistence. When the opportunity arose for a rapprochement between the US and China in the early 1970s, Mao Zedong and Zhou Enlai seized it.

From that time onwards, at least until the emergence of the US-led New Cold War in the last few years, China has been able to maintain peaceful and broadly cooperative, mutually-beneficial relations with the capitalist world, albeit with the complexities and contradictions that form an inevitable part of such a relationship.

With China's insertion into various global supply chains, it has become sufficiently important to the functioning of the global economy that the imperialist states have had to think very carefully about the wisdom of attacking or isolating it. Even now, when there exists a broad anti-China consensus in Washington, the US is struggling to make progress on "decoupling" or "delinking."

The Soviet Union – heroically – took on a heavy responsibility as the global centre of progressive forces, giving extensive practical solidarity to socialist states, national liberation movements and progressive governments around the world – including vast economic support to the People's Republic of China between 1949 and 1959; military and economic support to the people's democracies of Eastern Europe, to Cuba, Vietnam, Afghanistan, Angola, Nicaragua, Korea, Ethiopia and elsewhere; training, aid and weapons to the Palestine Liberation Organisation (PLO), the ANC in South Africa, Frelimo in Mozambique, SWAPO in South West Africa (now Namibia), PAIGC in Guinea Bissau, and others.

In addition to direct aid, the Soviet role as the protector of the progressive world – and its position as one of two 'superpowers' – meant that it felt forced to devote an extraordinary portion of its resources to military development. The figures vary wildly, but Russian-American historian Alexander Pantsov estimates that "at the start of Gorbachev's perestroika, in 1985, the Soviets were spending 40 percent of their budget on defence." Indeed Pantsov goes so far to conclude that "the economy of the USSR collapsed under the burden of military expenditures".[31] Certainly this was the objective of Ronald Reagan's 'full-court press' strategy in the early 1980s – vastly increasing US military expenditure, forcing the USSR to follow suit and thereby deepening its economic difficulties.

The arms race, the war in Afghanistan, and the much-needed support for progressive governments and liberation movements all took their toll on the Soviet economy.

China on the other hand has been able to enjoy a long period of peace. The Chinese People's Volunteer Army proved during the Korean War (the War to Resist America and Aid Korea) of 1950-53 that People's China was willing and able to defend itself from attack, and no doubt the US drew the appropriate lesson that any military operation against it would be highly risky.

The post-1978 leadership of the CPC realised the strategic potential of China's integration into the global economy. This could be thought of as a sort of strategic parity with Chinese characteristics – with a much lower price tag than its Soviet equivalent – and furthermore has enabled China to be a part of "the unprecedented global technological revolution, offering a short cut for the country to accelerate its industrial transformation and upgrade its economic structure."[32]

In this relatively secure international environment, China has been able to reduce its military spending from around 7 percent of GDP in 1978 to under 2 percent by the early 1990s (at which level it has remained),[33] allowing more resources to be devoted to improving living standards.

Although its strategy doesn't allow it to play an active military role in the defence of friendly states and movements, China's economic strength means that it is able to provide crucial support for progressive countries around the world. Deng in 1979 looked forward to a point in the future when China would be "a relatively wealthy country of the Third World with a per capita GNP of US$1,000", at which point "our people will enjoy a much higher standard of living than they do now" and "we could offer more assistance to the poor countries of the Third World".[34] This prediction has come true, and indeed been surpassed, and significantly impacts today's reality in Africa, Latin America, Central Asia, Southeast Asia, the Caribbean and the Pacific.

In the years since the Obama administration's *Pivot to Asia* (2011 onwards), and particularly since Donald Trump's trade war and escalation in anti-China rhetoric, which have not only continued but indeed been intensified during the Biden presidency, US-China relations have become increasingly tense, and the trajectory of mutually-beneficial cooperation starting in the early 1970s has been significantly eroded. However, China has used four decades of peace in order to make itself strong, and continues to be capable of defending itself without having to sacrifice the wellbeing of the people.

Conclusion

Reflecting in 1992 on the collapse of the Soviet Union and the European people's democracies, Deng urged people not to lose confidence in socialism:

> Feudal society replaced slave society, capitalism supplanted feudalism, and, after a long time, socialism will necessarily supersede capitalism. This is an irreversible general trend of historical development, but the road has many twists and turns. Over the several centuries that it took for capitalism to replace feudalism, how many times were monarchies restored! So, in a sense, temporary restorations are usual and can hardly be avoided. Some countries have suffered major setbacks, and socialism appears to have been weakened. But the people have been tempered by the setbacks and have drawn lessons from them, and that will make socialism develop in a healthier direction. So don't panic, don't think that Marxism has disappeared, that it's not useful any more and that it has been defeated. Nothing of the sort![35]

It is by now abundantly clear that the "end of history" predictions for China (and Cuba, Vietnam, Laos and the Democratic People's Republic of Korea) were well off the mark, notwithstanding Gordon Chang's regular divinations.[36]

China's reform process has been highly successful; the quality of life of its people continues to improve; it has emerged as a global leader in numerous key areas of science, technological innovation and environmental preservation; it is on the cusp of becoming a 'high income' country; and the Communist Party of China remains hugely popular, with a membership of close to a hundred million. In short, China is continuing to develop a form of socialism that is appropriate to its own conditions.

The CPC has been assiduous in learning from the Soviet demise in order to avoid suffering a similar fate. The US scholar David Shambaugh, citing a study by the Chinese Academy of Social Sciences, sums up some of the key lessons the CPC has tried to absorb. These include "concentrating on economic development and continuously improving people's standard of living", "upholding Marxism as the guiding ideology", "strengthening party leadership", and "continuously strengthening efforts on party building – especially in the areas of ideology, image, organisation, and democratic centralism – in order to safeguard the leadership power in the hands of loyal Marxists."[37]

The socialist project lives on in China, and becomes stronger every day. As quality of life gradually catches up with and outstrips the leading capitalist countries, and as China emerges as a global leader in science and technology and as a force for peace, multipolarity, sovereign development and environmental preservation, Chinese socialism will become more widely recognised as a highly effective, innovative and adaptive branch of Marxism, with an impact and significance extending well beyond its own national boundaries.

NOTES

1. Deng Xiaoping 1989, *With Stable Policies of Reform and Opening To the Outside World, China Can Have Great Hopes For the Future*, Marxist Internet Archive. https://www.marxists.org/reference/archive/deng-xiaoping/1989/127.htm
2. Fidel Castro 1992, *Castro Interviewed on Soviet Collapse, Stalin*, Castro Speech Data Base. http://lanic.utexas.edu/project/castro/db/1992/19920603.html
3. Xi Jinping, *The Governance of China. First edition*, Foreign Languages Press, Beijing, 2014, p24
4. Hu Angang, *China in 2020: A New Type of Superpower*, Brookings Institution Press, Washington DC, 2011, p28
5. Ha-Joon Chang, *Economics: The User's Guide*, Pelican, 2014, p75
6. Cit. Arne Odd Westad, *The Global Cold War: Third World Interventions and the Making of Our Times*, Cambridge University Press, 2011, p35
7. Michael Parenti, *Blackshirts & Reds: Rational Fascism & the Overthrow of Communism*, City Lights Books, 1997, p60
8. Jude Woodward, *The US vs China: Asia's New Cold War? Geopolitical Economy*, Manchester University Press, 2017, p248
9. Domenico Losurdo 2017, *Has China Turned to Capitalism? — Reflections on the Transition from Capitalism to Socialism*, International Critical Thought, 7(1), 15–31. https://doi.org/10.1080/21598282.2017.1287585
10. Kate Clark, *Twilight of the Soviet Union: Memoirs of a Moscow correspondent*, Bannister Publications, 2023, pp 7-8
11. Losurdo, *op cit*
12. Deng Xiaoping 1992, *Excerpts From Talks Given In Wuchang, Shenzhen, Zhuhai and Shanghai*, Marxist Internet Archive. https://www.marxists.org/reference/archive/deng-xiaoping/1992/179.htm
13. Martin Jacques, *When China Rules the World: The End of the Western World and the Birth of a New Global Order. 2. ed.*, Penguin Books, 2012, p176
14. Cit. Hu Angang, *China in 2020*, p33
15. Deng 1992, *op cit*
16. David Shambaugh, *China's Communist Party: Atrophy and Adaptation*, University of California Press, 2008, p65
17. Michael Roberts 2017, *The Russian revolution: some economic notes*, The Next Recession, https://thenextrecession.wordpress.com/2017/11/08/the-russian-revolution-some-economic-notes/.
18. *Rich countries attain record human development, but half of the poorest have gone backwards, finds UN Development Programme*, UN Development Programme. https://www.undp.org/china/press-releases/rich-countries-attain-record-human-development-half-poorest-have-gone-backwards-finds-un-development-programme

19 Deng Xiaoping 1989, *We Must Adhere To Socialism and Prevent Peaceful Evolution Towards Capitalism*, Marxist Internet Archive. https://www.marxists.org/reference/archive/deng-xiaoping/1989/173.htm
20 Cheng Enfu & Liu Zixu 2017, *The Historical Contribution of the October Revolution to the Economic and Social Development of the Soviet Union — Analysis of the Soviet Economic Model and the Causes of Its Dramatic End*, International Critical Thought, 7(3), 297–308. https://doi.org/10.1080/21598282.2017.1355143
21 Yegor Ligachev, *Inside Gorbachev's Kremlin: The Memoirs Of Yegor Ligachev*, Taylor & Francis, 2018, p286
22 Clark, *op cit*, p308
23 A useful source on this topic is: Domenico Losurdo, *Stalin: History and Critique of a Black Legend*. Translated by Henry Hakamäki and Salvatore Engel-Di Mauro. Authorized English edition. Iskra Books, 2023
24 Deng Xiaoping 1980, *Answers to the Italian Journalist Oriana Fallaci*, Selected Works of Deng Xiaoping. https://dengxiaopingworks.wordpress.com/2013/02/25/answers-to-the-italian-journalist-oriana-fallaci/
25 Fidel Castro 1989, *Discurso pronunciado por Fidel Castro Ruz en el acto de despedida de duelo a nuestros internacionalistas caídos durante el cumplimiento de honrosas misiones militares y civiles*, Cuba.cu. http://www.cuba.cu/gobierno/discursos/1989/esp/f071289e.html
26 Deng Xiaoping 1979, *Uphold the Four Cardinal Principles*, Marxist Internet Archive. https://www.marxists.org/reference/archive/deng-xiaoping/1979/115.htm
27 Xi Jinping 2013, *Correctly Deal With Both Historical Periods Before and After Reform and Opening Up*, China Copyright and Media. https://chinacopyrightandmedia.wordpress.com/2013/12/26/correctly-deal-with-both-historical-periods-before-and-after-reform-and-opening-up/
28 Xi Jinping, *The Governance of China*, Foreign Languages Press, 2014, p47
29 Xi Jinping 2021, *Speech at the Ceremony Marking the Centenary of the Communist Party of China*, Friends of Socialist China. https://socialistchina.org/2021/07/01/xi-jinpings-speech-on-the-centenary-of-the-communist-party-of-china/
30 Jacques, *op cit*, p277
31 Alexander Pantsov and Steven Levine, *Deng Xiaoping: A Revolutionary Life*, Oxford University Press, 2015, p432
32 Jenny Clegg, *China's Global Strategy: Towards a Multipolar World*, Pluto Press, 2009, p129
33 *Military expenditure (% of GDP) – China*, World Bank. https://data.worldbank.org/indicator/MS.MIL.XPND.GD.ZS?locations=CN

34 Deng Xiaoping 1979, *China's Goal Is To Achieve Comparative Prosperity By the End of the Century*, Marxist Internet Archive. https://www.marxists.org/reference/archive/deng-xiaoping/1979/87.htm
35 Deng 1992, *op cit*
36 The Chinese-American propagandist Gordon G Chang published his book *The Coming Collapse of China* in 2001, predicting the country's collapse by 2011.
37 David Shambaugh, *China's Communist Party: Atrophy and Adaptation*, University of California Press, 2008, p77

Contributors

Keith Bennett is a Co-editor of Friends of Socialist China. He studied Chinese History and Politics at SOAS University of London and, on graduating, began a lifetime of working with China at the Society for Anglo-Chinese Understanding (SACU) in 1979. He has visited China regularly since 1981 and is also Deputy Chairman of the 48 Group Club, whose July 1953 'Icebreaker Mission' was the first western trade delegation to the People's Republic.

Cheng Enfu is the former President of the Academy of Marxism, Chinese Academy of Social Sciences, member of the Chinese Academy of Social Sciences, Principal Professor at the University of Chinese Academy of Social Sciences, President of the World Association for Political Economy, Editor-in-Chief of the *World Review of Political Economy*, Editor-in-Chief of the *World Marxism Review*, and Honorary Editor-in-Chief of *International Critical Thought*. His research mainly focuses on Marxist political economy.

Dr Jenny Clegg is an independent writer and researcher, specialising in China's development and international role; and a former Senior Lecturer/Course Leader in Asia Pacific Studies at the University of Central Lancashire, Preston, UK. Her works include: *China's Global Strategy: towards a multipolar world* (Pluto Press,2009);

Storming the Heavens – Peasants and Revolution in China, 1925-1949: a Marxist perspective (Manifesto Press, forthcoming).

Kenny Coyle is a writer, editor and publisher. He is the director of Praxis Press and is a regular contributor to the *Morning Star*. He has lived and worked in various parts of Asia since 2000.

Michael Dunford is Emeritus Professor at the School of Global Studies, University of Sussex, and Affiliate Scholar at the Institute of Geographical Sciences and Natural Resources Research (IGSNRR), Chinese Academy of Sciences.

Radhika Desai is Professor at the Department of Political Studies, Director, Geopolitical Economy Research Group, University of Manitoba, Winnipeg, Canada and Convenor of the International Manifesto Group. Her *Geopolitical Economy: After US Hegemony, Globalization and Empire* (2013) proposed geopolitical economy as the proper Marxist anti-imperialist framework for understanding world affairs in the capitalist era. She hosts a fortnightly show, Geopolitical Economy Hour on the Geopolitical Economy Report website. Her most recent book is *Capitalism, Coronavirus and War: A Geopolitical Economy* (2022, Open Access).

Efe Can Gürcan is an Associate Professor who currently serves as a Visiting Senior Fellow at the London School of Economics and Political Science (LSE). Additionally, he holds the positions of Research Associate at the Geopolitical Economy

Research Group, based at the University of Manitoba, Visiting Scholar at the Shanghai University Institute of Global Studies, and Senior Research Fellow at Hainan CGE Peace Development Foundation. Gürcan has authored seven books and over 30 articles and book chapters on international development, international political economy, and political sociology. His latest co-authored book is *China on the Rise: The Transformation of Structural Power in the Era of Multipolarity* (Routledge, 2024).

Ken Hammond is professor of East Asian and Global History at New Mexico State University. He has been a socialist activist since his student days at Kent State University in the late 1960s-early '70s. He lived and worked in China from 1982-87 and has traveled and taught there over the past 42 years. He currently works with Pivot to Peace and is a member of the Party for Socialism and Liberation. He is the author of *China's Revolution and the Quest for a Socialist Future* and *China and the World, 1949-2024*.

Carlos Martinez is a researcher and political activist from London, Britain. His first book, *The End of the Beginning: Lessons of the Soviet Collapse*, was published in 2019 by LeftWord Books. His most recent book, *The East Is Still Red – Chinese Socialism in the 21st Century*, was published in 2023 by Praxis Press. He is a co-editor of Friends of Socialist China.

Andrew Murray is political correspondent of the Morning Star for the second time, the first being from 1978 to 1984. In between he has been Chair of the Stop the War Coalition, Chief of Staff at Unite the union, and an adviser to Jeremy Corbyn when he was Leader of the Labour Party. He has written many books including *The Fall and Rise of the British Left* and *Is Socialism Possible in Britain?*

J. Sykes is a member of the Freedom Road Socialist Organization and the author of *The Revolutionary Science of Marxism-Leninism*.

ESSENTIAL READING ON CHINA

China, after its revolution, has achieved the greatest improvement in life of the largest proportion of humanity of any country in history. In *China's Great Road*, John Ross explains how China achieved this step forward. His unequivocal conclusion is that socialism is responsible for this advance. *China's Great Road* analyses Chinese reality and argues socialists worldwide can learn from China.

Carlos Martinez argues in *The East is Still Red* that the decisive role of the Communist Party of China and its commitment to building 'socialism with Chinese characteristics' needs to be more widely understood especially in the West.

https://redletterspp.com/collections/china

OTHER PRAXIS PRESS TITLES

MAKING OUR OWN HISTORY by Jonathan White
A brilliant introduction to the Marxist approach to understanding and participating in social change.

MARX200
Leading scholars and activists from different countries – including Cuba, India and the UK – show that Marx's ideas continue to provide us with the analysis we need to understand our world today.

A PROMETHEAN VISION by Eric Rahim
"This small book is a very useful account of how Marx came to develop his materialist conception of history." Michael Löwy, *New Politics*

LINE OF MARCH by Max Adereth
A new edition of Max Adereth's historical analysis of British communism, focusing on the development of the party's various programmes. First published 1994.

1000 DAYS OF REVOLUTION
A fascinating account of the Allende Presidency, the dilemmas of peaceful and armed struggles for socialism, the role of US imperialism and domestic right-wing forces, and a self critical evaluation of the role of Chilean communists.

HARDBOILED ACTIVIST by Ken Fuller
A critical review of the work and politics of writer Dashiell Hammett, crime fiction legend, communist and staunch opponent of McCarthyism.

For more details, contact praxispress@me.com

ORDER online at www.redletterspp.com

www.ingramcontent.com/pod-product-compliance
Lightning Source LLC
Chambersburg PA
CBHW070332230426
43663CB00011B/2293